Eating Between the Lines

Eating Between the Lines

FOOD & EQUALITY IN AUSTRALIA

Rebecca Huntley

Published by Black Inc.,
an imprint of Schwartz Media Pty Ltd
Level 5, 289 Flinders Lane
Melbourne Victoria 3000 Australia
email: enquiries@blackincbooks.com
http://www.blackincbooks.com

The National Library of Australia
Cataloguing-in-Publication entry:

Huntley, Rebecca.
Eating between the lines :
food and equality in Australia
ISBN: 9781863952637 (pbk.)
Includes index.
Food--Social aspects--Australia. Food habits--
Australia. Food preferences--Australia.

641.30994

Index by Michael Ramsden
Book design by Thomas Deverall

Printed in Australia by Griffin Press

CONTENTS

To my sister, my mum and my nonna

INTRODUCTION: 'WELCOME TO AUSTRALIA!'

Thirty paces from my apartment there is a corner store. It calls itself a deli, but it is fooling no one. Run by an Asian couple, it stocks a sad selection of fruit and vegetables, a wide array of snack foods, salty and sweet, as well as overpriced canned goods and frozen meals. I go there when I find myself mid-recipe without milk or sugar. In its humming fridges and on its dusty shelves sit a few markers of eastern suburbs privilege – premium diet yoghurt, camembert, hummus and French jams. The rival store, separated from the first only by a shoe-repair place, is much the same, although the owners make fresh pork rolls and sell cumquats from their own garden. This store has imported Italian pasta sauce, Lean Cuisines and brie. A few steps further down the street there is an Italian café, where I regularly stop at 7 a.m. to grab coffee and raisin toast before I scoot to the bus. There, two Italian sisters serve fresh salads and sandwiches as well as pasta and meat dishes made daily by their very own *nonna*. Next to this café is a popular-with-the-locals Vietnamese restaurant. It is kitschy and cheerful, and my partner and I can eat heartily for less than twenty dollars. We often cart along a half-drunk bottle of wine or a few beers left over from a recent dinner party.

Walking up and down the stretch of shops where I live takes about ten minutes. It's not even the main shopping district in the area; five minutes' bus ride away, there is an enormous high-end mall that manages to draw me to it more often than I'd like. But my local neighbourhood is crammed with food options. There is a large café that serves a breakfast cassoulet that will keep you going until dinner; a Hungarian café serving a satisfying five-dollar salad and schnitzel roll; two chicken shops, one that proclaims all its chooks are cruelty and hormone free; a pizza place open from 10 a.m. to 1 a.m.; another deli café offering roast dinners on weeknights for twelve dollars, with children's meals half price; a second Vietnamese restaurant; a Thai restaurant that does a terrific beef salad; a cake store; a chocolate store; a fruit and vegetable store; two more trendy cafés that serve breakfast, lunch and dinner from Monday till Saturday; an organic vegan eatery; a health-food store that does lunches; a real deli that sells cheeses, small goods, fresh bread, organic meats and gelato; a pub and a leagues club, both of which offer counter meals and six-dollar steaks.

I can't claim that after a late night of work or play, I haven't succumbed to the greasy seductions of a supreme pizza or a quarter-chicken with chips. But in my neighbourhood, the variety and availability of healthy food is such that making the 'right' eating choices requires very little effort on my part.

*

Venturing thirty minutes by train westward to another suburb, you encounter a different eating world altogether. As I disembarked and exited the station, right in front of me was the quintessential Aussie take-away shop. Tepid roast chickens glistened under lights, lying side by side with kransky sausages, piles of hot chips, sausage rolls, pies and something you rarely see in my neck of the woods: Chiko Rolls. The fridge was full of chocolate bars, flavoured milk and soft-drinks hiding from the heat. The shop had a rack of sliced white bread (not a wholegrain to be found) as well as trays of eggs at three dollars a pop. Next door, a cheap Chinese take-away had closed down; phone books and unanswered mail waited for tables in the empty shop-front. I crossed the road and spotted another Chinese take-out; this one was usually open, although it was closed when I was visiting. It offered the familiar sweet and sour this, fried rice with that. A few metres away I found a hot-bread shop selling doughnuts, sausage rolls, pies and pasties, rolls and loaves of bread (a few with wholegrain). I came across a café whose sign promised sandwiches; peering through the window, I found it had joined its Oriental cousin and closed down. There was one bright spot in this neighbourhood, thanks to the presence of a large mosque close by. I walked into a Lebanese food store and bought a box of freshly baked date and pistachio biscuits. The store's owner watched me as I scanned the shelves full of cans of okra and tahini, jars of olives and fava beans, bottles of pomegranate molasses and rosewater, bags of walnuts and herbs. He was happy to chat with me about what I could do with these exotic ingredients. Here I could purchase a cheese pizza, with flat bread as the base, for $3.50. Other than a convenience store with a decent array of fruit, this was all this suburb had to offer me at lunchtime on a week day.

As I headed back to the train with my date biscuits in hand, I passed the take-away. A mother was buying hot chips for her preschool-aged son. She'd decided to draw the line at the kransky. 'You won't eat it,' she told him. As I crossed the road, a middle-aged woman in a dusky pink hijab was crossing the other way. An SUV slowed down as it neared her and I heard a man yell out, 'Welcome to Australia!'

The comparison between my street and this other cluster of shops in the west might seem unfair, even misleading. Certainly if I headed to the shopping strips of Lakemba or Footscray, Dandenong or Cabramatta, I would find more than just one decent food store, more than just meat pies and chocolate milk. Nevertheless, this simple comparison, this mere thirty-minute train ride from variety to gloom, begs the question – how fair is Australia's food culture?

*

Over the past decade we have seen a voracious demand for food media in all its forms. Australians have shown an almost inexhaustible appetite for cookbooks, magazines and novels featuring food and cooking.[1] Food magazines like *Good Taste*, *Delicious* and *Gourmet Traveller* out-sell popular women's and men's magazines, enjoying readership numbers of over half a million.[2] Cookbooks are now a fixture in the annual bestseller lists; in 2006 there were eight cookbooks in the top 100 sold that year.[3] We have also seen a boom in food television, both on free-to-air and cable, with food and cooking shows 'enjoying unprecedented popularity amongst diverse audiences, occupying prime-time slots in broadcasting scheduling, and becoming winners in the ratings game.'[4] The most obvious expression of this public food fascination is the phenomenon of the celebrity chef. Along with Jamie, Nigella and Gordon, we can boast a growing crop of home-grown celeb-chefs such as Bill Granger, Kylie Kwong, Donna Hay and Neil Perry, to name just a few. We see them on morning, midday and prime-time television, on the radio, in newspapers, on stage and, increasingly, on sauce jars and casserole dishes.

This enthusiasm for food and cooking among Australians comes as something of a surprise. Historically, as food historian Michael Symons points out, 'nobody has ever been terribly complimentary about Australian cuisine.'[5] Bush tucker aside, this country inherited as its founding food tradition the worst of British cooking. And yet, due mostly to subsequent waves of immigrants from good-eating countries and the bounty of our own land, we seem to have morphed from gastronomic backwater to culinary paradise. As early as 1976, then South Australian premier Don Dunstan was lauding our 'tremendous food resources' in his self-titled cookbook and declaring Australia 'the most fortunate country in the world for food.'[6] By the early nineties, food journalist Cherry Ripe announced that 'the food we are producing here … is currently some of the best in the world.'[7] In writing about our food today, there is a strong sense that Australian cuisine has 'come of age'[8] and, what's more, is garnering international accolades. In 2008, two Sydney restaurants, Tetsuya's and Rockpool, were ranked in the top fifty restaurants in the world (ninth and forty-ninth respectively) in *Restaurant* magazine's S. Pellegrino 'World's 50 Best Restaurants' list.[9]

No doubt the achievements of Australian chefs, restaurateurs, providores and industry leaders should be applauded. Nevertheless, I wonder how smug we can remain when we consider some unavoidable truths about food and eating in

Australia. The first is that although many of us are voracious consumers of food media, there is evidence we are cooking less than ever before. In addition, there are many who argue that we have seen a decline in general cooking skills, something usually blamed on the spread of pre-prepared foods, modern technologies and the increased busyness of people both at home and at work.[10]

The second unavoidable truth is one that has attracted much media attention, political comment and public concern – that is, the rising rates of obesity among Australian adults and children. In 2008, one study found that Australia had overtaken the United States as the world's most obese nation.[11] Policy-makers and politicians fret over the dramatic jump in obesity rates because the cost of obesity, to both the public and the private sectors, is significant. In October 2006, Access Economics prepared a report on the economic costs of obesity, particularly obesity-related diseases such as diabetes type 2, cardio-vascular diseases, osteoarthritis and certain cancers. They estimated that the direct financial cost of obesity in 2005 was $3.767 billion. This included productivity costs of $1.7 billion, health-system costs of $873 million and carer costs of $804 million. In addition, there were what are fittingly called 'dead weight losses' from such things as taxation revenue foregone, welfare and other government payments of $358 million, and other indirect costs calculated at $40 million. The net cost of lost wellbeing was valued at a further $17.2 billion, bringing the total cost of obesity in 2005 to $21.0 billion.[12]

Obesity is a worldwide problem, one to which the World Health Authority (the WHO) is paying increasing attention. The WHO states on its website that:

> Obesity is one of today's most blatantly visible – yet most neglected – public health problems. Paradoxically coexisting with under-nutrition, an escalating global epidemic of overweight and obesity – 'globesity' – is taking over many parts of the world.[13]

In 2005, the WHO estimated that there were around 1.6 billion adults who were overweight and at least 400 million adults who were obese. This was double the number of obese people the WHO had estimated a decade previously.[14] Childhood obesity is also a global problem; in 2005, the WHO estimated at least 20 million children were overweight.

I am not a health expert, but something tells me that obese Australians, like their counterparts in developed and developing countries, haven't become obese eating Tetsuya's dégustation menu, or even from dining in the kinds of Italian cafés and Vietnamese restaurants in my neighbourhood. As the WHO states, the problem is chiefly caused by 'a global shift in diet towards increased intake of energy-dense foods that are high in fat and sugars but low in vitamins, minerals and other micronutrients.' This new diet works to the detriment of all when combined with the increasingly sedentary nature of work, changing modes of transport and increasing urbanisation.

In this country, a sharp contrast can be observed. On the one hand there is the brilliant food of celebrity chefs exhibited in glossy food publications and engaging TV shows. Then there is the reality of Australia's obesity statistics, the reliance of increasingly busy people on pre-packaged and pre-prepared food, and the evidence that we watch people cook more than we cook ourselves. All of which leads me to question the extent to which our food media, celebrity chefs and internationally acclaimed restaurants have improved the way Australians eat on a daily basis. British food journalist Joanna Blythman would endorse my scepticism. In *Bad Food Britain* she rejects outright the idea that the average Briton's diet has been improved by Nigella and her ilk. She contests the idea that there has been any celebrity-chef-led food revolution:

> Nation of foodies! Food revolution! Who are we kidding? British eating habits are getting worse, not better ... Britain likes to see itself nowadays as a fully functioning, participatory food culture. In truth, this vision is a chimera, an unconvincing construction built on talking up by the media, the chattering classes ... and TV chefs on the make.[15]

In Blythman's view, the cool-food Britannia story ignores some important facts, such as the nation's growing addiction to industrial foods (Britain eats 51 per cent of all the savoury snacks and crisps consumed in Europe), the decline in cooking skills and cooking generally, the poor diet of children and the growing obesity problem.[16] 'Britain lives in a fantasy food world, a virtual food state,' populated by 'food voyeurs,' Blythman argues. While British bookshelves and TV schedules might be full of good food, the same cannot be said of British fridges and larders. 'The more media space food and cooking occupies in Britain, the less it reflects any grass roots practical activity,' Blythman writes.[17] Blythman is particularly vitriolic in her assessment of celebrity chefs, arguing that they are merely circus performers juggling whisks and

8

carrots, appealing to people who have little or no interest in food and cooking.[18] I am not sure I entirely agree with her on this point. While it is easy to dismiss cooking shows as 'foodatainment' and 'gastro-porn,' they can serve to educate viewers.[19] As writer Marian Halligan argues, at least fans of these cooking shows are 'looking at, even if they aren't eating, interesting food.'[20] It's a start, and perhaps one day interest might lead to action. What is clear, however, is that watching endless cooking shows and subscribing to *Gourmet Traveller* isn't going to help you into the kitchen if your lifestyle, and the social and economic conditions that shape it, don't allow you the requisite time, money or access to good-quality ingredients.

In her analysis of the woeful eating habits of her countrymen, Blythman concludes that Britain is 'a strange and aberrant' land, 'a cultural exception in Europe and second only to the US in its capacity to shock outsiders with its eating habits.'[21] In making this argument, she quotes London-based Australian food writer Terry Durack, who wrote the following in a British newspaper:

> As an Australian, I often find myself blinking in disbelief at the average Briton's relationship with food, at how unimportant it is to so many people. But then, I grew up in a country where good food was available to all at a good price.[22]

Durack's claim that Australians eat better than the British may well be true. The British food bar is pretty low, so it's no great achievement that we can clear it. However, I don't believe we can be confident of the truth of Durack's claim that good food is available to all Australians at a good price. Not all of us live in a lucky eating country. And the top-class food familiar to critics like Durack is not the kind of food the vast majority of Australians have the time, money or opportunity to enjoy. A quick review of data on what Australians buy in supermarkets confirms this. For those interested in the food habits of so-called 'ordinary Australians,' research firm AC Nielsen's list of the top 100 most purchased products is illuminating reading. According to this list, we are very fond of Coca-Cola, Tip Top bread, Cadbury's chocolates, instant coffee, Yoplait yoghurt, Peter's ice-cream, frozen vegetables, Bega cheese, crisps, canned fish and Arnott's biscuits.[23] Not a pesto, sourdough baguette or laksa paste to be found.

It's not my neighbourhood, with its vegan sushi and eggs Florentine, that we need to visit to understand Australia's eating habits. It's the second suburb I went to, with its hot chips and white bread, its convenience stores and closed-down cafés. To that extent, the xenophobe in the SUV was right. This is Australia.

This book is a different kind of food tour. It will show that how, what and when we eat reveals much about our society, and about who amongst us is getting the biggest slice of the pie.

CHEAP AS CHIPS

Munno Para shopping centre can easily be spotted as you drive up Main North Road through the suburbs of Elizabeth and Smithfield. You'd pass the place if you were heading north from Adelaide to sample the wine and food of the famous Barossa Valley. Apparently 'Munno Para' means 'golden wattle creek' in the Kaurna dialect. It wasn't the season for wattle flowers, though, and I saw no evidence of a creek; just an enormous concrete column reaching for the sky, hailing the existence of the centre. Here is where I can observe (or so I am told by an Adelaide acquaintance) real 'Elizabethans.' The newly renovated Elizabeth shopping centre is about ten minutes away from Munno Para and boasts a Myer department store and a cinema. The new centre is up-market compared to the daggier and reputedly more authentic local stomping ground of Munno Para.

The 2006 census figures reveal some salient facts about this corner of Australia.[1] The census data tells us that the overwhelming majority of residents born overseas living in Elizabeth come from England, Scotland or Wales. This is unsurprising considering Elizabeth was established as a satellite town in the mid fifties and was a magnet for British migrants. The average weekly income for an Elizabethan in 2006 was $347 (a mere $100 above the official poverty line) compared to the national average of $466. Weekly household and family incomes are even more disparate.[2] There is a high concentration of one-parent families in Elizabeth[3] and an even higher concentration of Elizabethans living in public housing.[4] Elizabeth has one of the highest unemployment rates in South Australia, as well as a high youth unemployment rate.[5] In his first speech as a federal parliamentarian, local member David Fawcett described communities like Elizabeth, Salisbury and Munno Para as beset with 'intergenerational unemployment' and 'social challenges'; in these communities, teachers are 'dealing with children who, for example, come to school with no breakfast or perhaps no support in early learning.'[6]

It's best to drive to and around Munno Para. When this area was first established, there was no train line connecting these areas to Adelaide; there is one now and some bus routes are operating, but it's still not great for public transport. Nor is it particularly amenable to walking or cycling. The drive from Adelaide's city centre takes you through affluent suburbs, then through less affluent ones and then quickly you find yourself on the outskirts of the city. Development is patchy. There are occasional strips of shops, which often include discount stores loudly proclaiming the insanity of their owners. The housing company Delfin is building a development at Mawson Lakes, an 'energetic mix of education, recreation, retail, residential and commercial facilities,' according to its website. The cost of a house in this area is around $350,000, well above the region's average house price of around $250,000.

Munno Para shopping centre is visible not just for its thrusting sign, but also for the lurid ring of fast-food outlets that surrounds it: Red Dragon Chinese, Hungry Jack's, McDonald's, Red Rooster, Pizza Hut and Barnacle Bill's (a South Australian fish and chip chain I recall from my childhood for its deep-fried pineapple rings). Turning into Munno Para's parking lot, finding a park and getting out of the passenger seat, I noticed a half-eaten box of chicken-flavoured crisps next to a baby chair in the sedan next to me. Walking into the centre, I side-stepped to avoid the hot chips mashed into the pavement, only to be hit by a wave of cigarette smoke created by a clutch of centre workers and visitors hanging around the electronic doors.

In terms of shopping, the small centre is dominated by discount stores such as Spotlight, Go-Lo, Cheap as Chips and the biggest Millers 'Family Fashion for Less' store I have ever seen. There were racks of five-dollar shirts outside many of these shops and in the lingerie store I spied something incredibly rare: Elle Macpherson lace lingerie in extra large, front and centre in the window display. There were more than a couple of plus-size stores as well.

Food is the other dominant presence in the centre. When I was there, it was nearly lunchtime on a weekday and the numerous food outlets were doing a brisk trade: Subway, Donut King, Wendy's and various Asian and Italian fastfood offerings. I stopped outside Tone's Snack Foods to peruse their 'Health Menu,' which included a few sandwiches, one with chicken, cheese, avocado and mayonnaise for $6.10, and a ham and cheese croissant for $4.50. No fruit salad or regular salad to be seen. More importantly, the health menu was more expensive than the standard one, which offered an alluring egg and bacon roll for $4.10 and a generous burger with the lot for $5.90. The centre does contain a decent fruit and veg shop, a yoghurt store, a juice store and a health-food store (in front of which were display tables full of products for diabetes and weight loss). But these outlets were eclipsed by shops and stalls selling the worst kind of take-away.

If you tire of shopping and eating at Munno Para, you can play 'The Chocoholic Game.' I counted three of these machines scattered around the centre. It is one of those arcade games involving a booth full of chocolate bars and an electronic hand that you manoeuvre to pick up the sweets: a dollar for three plays or two dollars for seven plays. There was adult gambling available, too: a TAB, a community bingo stall and a stall selling lucky dips for lottery tickets (twenty-five cents for a chance to win fifty dollars). All were doing good business.

It was lunchtime and I was getting hungry, but I decided to drive the forty minutes or so back to the suburbs of salad. I was beginning to feel as if I was gaining weight just walking Munno Para's well-worn concrete floors.

*

Munno Para could easily be described as an 'obesogenic environment.' This is an environment with a concentration of fast-food outlets to the exclusion of other food options, a place that encourages the over-consumption of foods high in fat and sugar. They also tend to be places that hinder physical activity, planned in such a way as to ensure residents are reliant on their cars; there are few safe and attractive public places for exercise. In Australia, obesogenic environments like Munno Para are usually located in areas of relative economic deprivation, in suburbs on the fringes of our major cities. These are suburbs where, as journalist Christine Jackman observes, 'the only shopping centre within walking distance boasts a liquor store, a Chinese take-away and a McDonald's – but the fruit and vegetable shop has closed down.'[7]

There is substantial Australian and international research showing strong correlations between weight, place and social disadvantage.[8] In other words, there is a higher risk of overweight and obesity among residents of areas of social disadvantage such as Munno Para and Elizabeth. The clear social gradient to obesity in Australia was acknowledged in a report released in late 2003 by the Australian Institute of Health and Welfare (AIHW) entitled 'Are All Australians Gaining Weight?' That report found that while the rise in obesity was widespread, touching virtually all socio-demographic groups, it was not 'randomly distributed':

> Those most likely to be obese are poor, indigenous and living outside metropolitan areas … The most vulnerable groups are aged between 45 and 64 in the most disadvantaged socio-economic group: men and women without post-school qualifications, the lowest incomes and indigenous people.[9]

The nexus between socio-economic disadvantage and obesity in women is particularly acute. The AIHW found that women in the most disadvantaged socio-economic group had nearly double the rate of obesity (22.6 per cent) of those in the most advantaged group (12.1 per cent). Rates of overweight also varied considerably between the two groups: 46.8 per cent and 37.6 per cent respectively.[10] The lower a woman's socio-economic status, the more likely she is to be obese. Hence the bigger market for extra-large lingerie in Munno Para.

It's not easy to account for the social gradient to obesity. Why, for example, is there a stronger correlation between obesity and social disadvantage in women than in men? For some it might be tempting to assume that people living in poverty are ignorant about how to eat properly. Yet, as health researcher Cate Burns points out, knowing about nutrition and healthy eating doesn't automatically ensure you will eat healthier.[11] Education isn't always the silver bullet we imagine it to be. Maybe low-income families know what's healthy but don't care? Not necessarily so. Burns points to numerous international and some domestic studies that have shown that low-income families are just as concerned about health and nutrition as those from higher socio-economic backgrounds.[12]

Basically, we have a poor understanding of the factors that contribute to unhealthy eating and obesity in low-income groups. And our understanding of the problem is also more than a little tainted by preconceived notions about both fat people and poor people. In our culture (as in the United Kingdom and the United States), being fat is often associated with being poor. Fat is seen as a marker of low social status in these cultures. The fat body is a body that has been created by bad food, bad lifestyle and bad choices, which we often view as synonymous with the underclass. Consider, for example, the moment in Jonathan Franzen's novel *The Corrections* when the eldest son, Gary, describes his feelings of bourgeois disgust as he observes the suburban poor waddling around a local shopping mall:

Poor people smoked. Poor people ate Krispy Kreme doughnuts by the dozen. Poor people practiced poor hygiene and lived in toxic neighbourhoods … They were a dumber, sadder, fatter, and more resignedly suffering breed.[13]

Franzen's novel is set in the United States, but the same sentiments apply to Australia, America's rival in the fat stakes. Poor people are those types we see on *Today Tonight*, trashing public housing, cheating the welfare system and arguing with their neighbours. They wear grotty sweatshirts and trackpants. And the most obvious sign of their poverty? They are fat.

When poor people are fat, it confirms our worse prejudices about them – that they are ill-disciplined, anti-social, lacking in confidence and taste. The idea that fatness indicates sickness or weakness of character is not entirely new.[14] As anti-globalisation activist and author Raj Patel comments, 'Every culture has had, in some form or other, an understanding of our bodies as public ledgers on which is written the catalogue of our private vices.'[15] As a consequence, for those who seek to avoid moral judgements in their analysis of social trends and human behaviour, the evident social gradient to obesity is difficult to discuss. You can inadvertently feed into the stereotype that poor equals fat equals lazy.

Setting aside these assumptions about the poor, it seems natural to consider that cost may be the cause of the less-than-healthy eating habits of those in the lowest quintiles. Does eating well cost more than eating badly? This continues to be the perception amongst some consumers and food experts, but the matter is by no means settled. There are those in the nutrition profession who maintain that healthy eating needn't be more expensive and can in fact cost less. These critics of the 'eating junk is cheaper' thesis tend to focus on other factors, namely people's cooking skills, facilities, time, tastes and motivation, which they argue might vary across social groups.[16]

On the other hand, Cate Burns points to numerous studies that show that energy-dense foods offer the 'most dietary energy at the lowest cost' and are thus a tempting choice for individuals and families on restricted incomes. Advising low-income consumers, Burns argues, to replace fat and sweets with fresh fruit and vegetables ignores the economic appeal of the former.[17] Developments in agriculture and food technology have ensured that these energy-dense foods can be produced at a lower energy cost than, for example, fruits and vegetables. Energy-dense foods are those that contain a large number of calories from sugar and fat in only a small amount of food: chocolate, cake, biscuits, pizza and soft-drinks, for instance. Energy cost refers to the amount of money required to plant, harvest, store, transport preserve and prepare food. In the United States the energy cost of potato chips is about twenty cents, whereas that of fresh carrots is ninety-five cents. The energy cost of a soft-drink is thirty cents; for orange juice from concentrate, it is $1.43.[18] As the Australian drought worsens, we might expect a similar situation here.

In a paper published in the *Health Promotion Journal of Australia* in late 2006, researchers from the New South Wales Department of Health found that for one in five households in the poorest suburbs of Sydney's south west, healthy food remains something of a luxury, owing mostly to increasing costs. As part of an article about the study, journalists Julie

Robotham and Kerry Coleman interviewed a mother of two, Amanda Thomas, a resident of the south-western suburbs dependent on Centrelink payments to survive. Thomas told the reporters that the increasing cost of fruit and veggies meant she had to rely on cheap, processed foods and couldn't afford to buy the grapes her four-year-old loved because they cost $14.99 a kilo. 'The kids get taught how to eat healthy at playgroup but I can't afford to back that up and feed them those foods at home,' Thomas explained.[19]

*

I wanted to conduct my own, albeit limited, test of whether healthy food was necessarily more expensive to buy than unhealthy alternatives. Like Munno Para, my local shopping centre is full of food options, albeit pretty good ones as it is slap-bang in the middle of the affluent eastern suburbs of Sydney. First, I ventured into one of the food halls in the centre. What healthy choices were on offer? I could buy a vegeburger with tabouli, hummus and tasty cheese for $7.10 or a turkey-breast sandwich with salad for $8.30. But if I was on a budget, I would save dollars and cents by going for the KFC Works Burger for $5.45 or the Oporto Bondi Burger for $5.98.

I then headed down to the supermarket on the centre's lowest level to compare the cost of different food staples. Good news in the dairy department: there was no difference whatsoever in the price of full-fat and low-fat milk or light and normal tasty cheese. There was very little difference between the cost of two litres of unrefrigerated orange juice (no sugar added) and two litres of orange cordial, maybe about twenty cents. However, things changed when I moved on to other kinds of foods. Diet mince-meat (with very little fat) was $13.99 a kilo compared to normal mince for $8.99, speckled with fat. If you wanted a microwave dinner, there was also a low-fat mark-up of sorts. A single serve of frozen bacon and mushroom pasta was $3.18; Lean Cuisine's mushroom pasta cost $4.99. Thick white bread (the kind kids love) was $3.49 for 650 grams compared to $4.35 for a loaf of soy and linseed bread, reputedly beneficial for older women. And what if you wanted to prepare an entire family meal for two adults and two kids? If you decided to go all CSIRO Diet, you could feed a family of four with lean lamb rump steaks ($11.76 for six), pumpkin ($2.71 per half) and broccolini ($2.78 for two) for around twenty dollars. However, if you opted for sausages ($3.79 for eight), fries ($2.49 for 750 grams) and baked beans (89 cents for two) you could satisfy them for around eight dollars.

Everywhere I looked, healthy food ended up being, at best, the same cost as the full-fat or unhealthy choice and, at worst, significantly more expensive. In putting together these hypothetical meals, of course, I might be accused of comparing apples with oranges; it may well be possible to pull together a cheaper healthy meal than the one imagined here. Across the board, however, fattier cuts of meat and canned foods are generally cheaper than lean meat and fresh fruit and vegetables. It's hard to know whether this is because the healthier foods are more expensive to produce, or because food manufacturers know that those on high incomes are willing and able to pay more for healthy food.

Cost isn't the only factor at work here. Returning to the notion of 'obesogenic environments,' we can see that cost is just one element at play in a range of forces that influence peoples' food 'choices.'[20] Is it possible that the lifestyles of the socially disadvantaged are in part conditioned by different, class-based perceptions about what constitutes overweight? There is little doubt that what constitutes 'fat' if you are working as a beauty editor at *Vogue* magazine may be kilos away from what constitutes 'fat' if you are a check-out chick at Bi-Lo in Elizabeth. Is the sheer concentration of fast-food outlets in places like Munno Para a contributing factor? Associations have been found between economic deprivation and density of fast-food outlets in poorer neighbourhoods. In Melbourne, for example, poorer suburbs are home to around 2.5 times more fast-food outlets than are affluent areas.[21] If you are surrounded by fast food, perhaps it becomes the eating norm. Or maybe, as academic Michael Gard and others have suggested, the poor are unhealthier than the rich because they have more to worry about, with 'healthy eating' coming a poor second to 'just surviving.'[22] Combine all this with the fact that there may well be fewer safe places in low socio-economic areas to walk or exercise. Due to inadequate public transport, residents in these areas may also rely heavily on cars to get to and from work, shops and family, cutting down on any possible incidental exercise involved in walking to and from the bus stop and shops.

So, other than cost, there are a range of environmental factors that can contribute to the lifestyle patterns of people who live in places like Munno Para.[23] This in and of itself won't guarantee the poor will be fat. Genetics, family and personality will also play a part. It seems that living in such a suburb, however, can make the right food and lifestyle decisions even harder to make than they normally are.

*

It is easy to forget, with all the focus on fat and overeating and diets, that there are still Australians who go hungry, who wonder where their next meal is coming from: the homeless, the destitute, the uncared-for elderly.[24] We are a food-secure nation, but there are those of us (somewhere between 7 and 10 per cent of the population) who live with food insecurity every day.[25] This includes the one child in five who lives in relative poverty and is going without meals because of lack of money.[26] These are the kinds of statistics we don't hear enough about, consumed as we are with record levels of employment and growth in the last decade of economic prosperity.

It is somewhat ironic that while Australians are getting fatter, we as a society are becoming no more accepting of fat people. There remains that sense of disgust described in Franzen's novel; we still see the fat body as a blubbery manifestation of moral and social degradation. Note the popularity of reality TV shows like *The Biggest Loser*, where viewers get to enjoy the thrill of watching the obese stripped down to their underwear and weighed in public, tortured by exercise until they are red and sweaty and sometimes weeping, subjected to cruel 'tests' involving smorgasbords of sweets and junk foods. It's like a cross between sumo wrestling and bear-baiting, and yet we lap it up, perhaps because we think the victims deserve their plight. It seems to me that the tendency to blame fat people for their own physical condition neatly matches our growing tendency to blame poor people for their place at the bottom of the social scale.

FAT KIDS

One Friday afternoon, as I stepped out of the crowded carriage onto Platform 3, I locked eyes with a young girl. She and her mother were waiting to board the train westward. The girl looked about three years old to me but she could have been younger. It was hard to tell. She was sitting in a stroller or, more accurately, wedged in. She was big. Not big-boned, but fat. Not baby fat, but actually fat. On the little food tray in front of her, I spotted a half-eaten Happy Meal: a small serve of fries spilling from its greasy paper envelope and the remnants of a Junior Burger. I looked up to see her mother holding what must have been the soft-drink component of the meal deal. As the girl kept staring at me, I thought to myself, 'What is that woman doing, feeding her kid that junk?' As I climbed the stairs, I checked my attitude. Who was I to judge her situation? I didn't know the family and its circumstances and so on. But the impulse to condemn parents (particularly mothers, who are usually the family food gatekeepers) can be irresistible.

In recent years, fat kids have been a popular topic with the Australian media, particularly op-ed columnists. Searching the *Age* and the *Sydney Morning Herald* websites for the terms 'children' and 'obesity' uncovers a mere five stories published in 1996, compared to 133 stories in 2006. Academics Michael

Gard and Jan Wright found similar results in a media search for their book *The Obesity Epidemic*.[1] Much of this press coverage verges on the exaggerated, even the hysterical. One newspaper article describes academic research on forty-three children 'who are so obese they can hardly move.'[2] Another gives the nation a deadline of five years to 'rein in' child obesity (as if it were a plague or virus).[3] It's not uncommon for these stories to describe the rise in the number of overweight and obese children as a 'crisis' or an 'epidemic.' It's not just the media who invoke the language of contagion. Consider the following introduction to a 2004 briefing from the Australian government's Institute of Health and Welfare, entitled 'A Rising Epidemic':

> Rates of obesity are rising alarmingly in many parts of the world, and this trend is not restricted to adults. Child and adolescent obesity is a significant health problem. In Australia, the prevalence of obesity in children and adolescents has jumped markedly in all age groups and for both boys and girls over the past few decades.[4]

Is there an epidemic of fat kids in Australia? Or simply an epidemic of the use of the term 'epidemic' to describe what's happening to the waistlines of Australian children?

Some commentators argue that childhood obesity has been (pardon the joke) blown out of all proportion. According to Catharine Lumby and Duncan Fine, authors of *Why TV is Good for Kids*, the hand wringing over childhood obesity is a moral panic, pure and simple. They point to the problems inherent in the way overweight is calculated using the

Body Mass Index (BMI). They point out that the BMI is a one-size-fits-all measurement that can't accommodate different body types, ethnicities or individuals.[5] Gard and Wright argue in a similar vein, stating that 'when the prevailing conditions are described as an 'epidemic,' hyperbole no longer looks like hyperbole, ideology can look like common sense and moralising can even look like science.'[6] I sometimes think 'moral panic' is as overused a term as 'epidemic.' In order to prove an important point, Lumby, Gard *et al* tend to downplay the increased prevalence of overweight and obese kids. And even the most sober analysts recognise that there *has* been an increase that merits parental, public and political concern. What has that increase been?

Before we even start to examine the available statistics, it's important to appreciate that measuring obesity in children can be difficult, owing in part to differences in developmental rates and maturation. Furthermore, the most recent and reliable national data on the prevalence of obesity in Australian children and adolescents comes from two surveys that are long-in-the-tooth to say the least: the 1985 Australian Health and Fitness Survey (AHFS) and the 1995 National Nutrition Survey (NNS). What those surveys found was that in the ten-year period from 1985 to 1995 the prevalence of obesity among seven-to-fifteen-year-olds tripled. According to government data from the 1995 survey, one in five children was found to be overweight or obese.[7]

The most recent data on childhood obesity comes from state-based surveys, most of which show increases in the level of the problem since 1995. For example, a 2000 survey of New South Wales primary school children aged seven to eleven found that 26.2 per cent of boys and 28.4 per cent of girls surveyed were overweight, while the prevalence of obesity was reported at 9.9 per cent of boys and 7.1 per cent of girls. The 2003 Sentinel Site for Obesity Prevention in Victoria study reported that 26.7 per cent of seven-to-eleven-year-olds surveyed were classed as overweight, while 7.9 per cent were classed as obese. Data from South Australia indicates that obesity may be developing at a much younger age, with recent research showing the percentage of obese pre-schoolers (children aged four years) in that state rose from 3.5 per cent for girls and 3.2 per cent for boys in 1995 to 5.8 per cent for girls and 4.1 per cent for boys in 2002.[8]

So while the general trend, according to these surveys, is towards our kids getting fatter, there are gaps in our knowledge and qualifications apply when we attempt to measure the problem. 'Overweight' and 'obese' are often lumped together in these statistics and in media reporting of them, but there is a significant difference between an overweight child and an obese child. We hear both words, but perhaps 'obese' rings most loudly in our ears. It conjures up a flock of school kids squeezed into their uniforms, lumbering from car to school, lunchboxes overflowing with Tiny Teddies and packets of chips.

I hoped to get a more accurate picture from those who actually deal with these issues every day. So I drove south to Wollongong Hospital to talk to Jane Cleary, one of a small number of paediatric dieticians working in the New South Wales health system. Wollongong Hospital services the Illawarra region, reaching out to well-to-do postcodes such as Sandon Point, picturesque costal towns such as Wombarra and Thirroul as well as socially disadvantaged areas such as

Nowra and Dapto. Jane's patients span the whole spectrum: she deals with pregnant mums, babies and children up to eighteen years old. She treats kids with allergies, with disabilities, with eating disorders as well as those who are overweight and obese. Some of Jane's work is in-house, with patients who have been referred to her by doctors and paediatricians, but she also works in the community. When I arrived to interview her, Jane introduced me to her boss, Marijana Milosavljevic, who heads the nutrition and dietetics department at the hospital. Marijana has been a nutritionist for over twenty years, including a stint in Elizabeth in South Australia. Both women are working parents: Jane has two kids under twelve and Marijana two teenagers and a primary-schooler.

For Marijana, the media focus on childhood obesity is too broad-brush in its approach to be particularly useful. 'There is a real problem with obesity amongst children,' Marijana told me, 'but not across all groups. It's really concentrated in lower socio-economic groups.' Ironically, both Jane and Marijana believe these are often the hardest groups for them to access – or the ones most reluctant to seek guidance and support. 'The kids who come to me are generally from pretty middle-class backgrounds,' Jane explained. 'Their parents understand the health system and are already seeing a paediatrician. They feel confident to ask for help.' Marijana believes the picture is complicated by ethnicity as well as socio-economic disadvantage. 'There is some reluctance amongst particular migrant groups to access mainstream health services. There are certain cultural norms at work too, such as the belief that larger children equate to healthier adults.'

In the course of our discussion, Jane and Marijana mentioned the work of Dr Jenny O'Dea, an expert in obesity in children and teenagers working at the University of Sydney. In 2000, O'Dea conducted a national nutritional study of 4441 students from thirty-eight schools randomly selected from lists of all state and territory schools in Australia. Public, private and Catholic schools, in both rural and urban areas, were represented. The results showed that children attending schools categorised as being of low socio-economic status were likely to be shorter and fatter than their peers at schools from the middle and high socio-economic classes. O'Dea concluded that socio-economic status is a factor in the development of overweight and obesity in Australian children.[9] This conclusion is confirmed by data on children from other socially disadvantaged groups.[10] ABS statistics show that indigenous youth, like their parents, are more likely to be overweight or obese than non-indigenous kids.[11] The role disadvantage plays in the rising rates of overweight and obese Australian children is often overlooked, both in media accounts of an obesity 'epidemic' and in commentary that claims this is all just a 'moral panic.'

Another researcher coming to similar conclusions is Dr Helen Truby. Helen is a fellow at the Children's Nutrition Centre in Brisbane, one of the leading paediatric nutrition research centres in Australia. She has a background in dietetics and started her career working in the Children's Hospital in Melbourne. When we met, she was looking at dietary manipulation in children – how altering the levels of fat, protein and carbohydrates in their diets might affect their weight. I visited her at the centre one crisp Brisbane morning and asked her the kinds of questions I had posed to Jane and Marijana. Can the increasing number of overweight and obese children rightly be described as an epidemic? 'It is fairly accurate,' Truby responded, 'although the word "epidemic" implies it is catching, which it isn't. But in terms of the numbers, the problem in Australia is accelerating.' However, like Jane Cleary, Truby believes that the problem is worsening in some groups of kids but not others. Truby's clients also tend to come from higher up the socio-economic scale. 'A number of people who come to us are very middle class. They know how to access our kinds of services quite easily.' It's a different case for single parents. 'They haven't got medical insurance, they don't really know how to access our services, and these are the people we really need to reach out to.' In Truby's experience there is a social gradient to obesity in children, as there is in adults:

These single parents and disadvantaged families are often the most difficult to work with because there are numerous constraints on their lifestyle. Health is not really a priority. It's all about survival from day-to-day. Just keeping the family going, bringing in some money each week, is a challenge. We have to get them to come into the hospital and transport issues can sometimes prove difficult. They have to get a referral from a GP and that can cost you twenty dollars or more. I don't think we are accessing those people who need it the most.

In Truby's experience, kids from Pacific Islander families are also at risk of becoming overweight and obese. 'They are genetically predisposed to diabetes. It's a combination of genetics and lifestyle. They have a high-carb diet based mainly around rice and huge serving sizes.' Why is there this social gradient to obesity in kids? 'Those in socially disadvantaged families have fewer opportunities to make healthy choices,' Truby explained. 'If you go to the supermarket you can get ten doughnuts for $1.99 whereas you can get four apples for that amount. What choices are you going to make? These are also families who are less likely to join a sports club or be involved in organised activities out of the home. It is cheaper to watch TV.'

*

In *The Obesity Epidemic*, Gard and Wright argue that much of the research and commentary on obesity and children fits neatly into 'the familiar story of Western decadence and decline.'[12] The obesity epidemic, we are told, is the consequence of modern life, our reliance on technology, industrialised foods, labour-saving devices and our quick-fix, want-it-all-now ethos. Children in particular have been singled out as a problematic lot. Experts of one kind or another regularly describe today's children as not only fatter than previous generations, but also less active, less athletically skilled, less interested in physical activity, less self-disciplined and more addicted to technology.[13] In this way, the youngest members of our society come to personify our worst tendencies as a culture: undisciplined and lazy, materialistic and greedy, in the thrall of technology and advertising. Childhood obesity provides a pretext for social commentators of all political stripes (myself included) to discuss whatever social or moral issue is *really* on their minds: the decline of family values, the corruptive influence of the media, the social devastation caused by divorce, the negligence of working mothers, the evils of feminism, of advertising, of packaged foods, of overwork and so on. As Gard and Wright suggest, because public discussion of the obesity epidemic 'does not differentiate between particular social groups, it creates the perfect context in which people can talk vaguely about the "environment" or "society," "Western societies" or "modern lifestyles" or simply "we.'"[14] Childhood obesity: what lies beneath?

As food historian Margaret Visser points out, our relationship to food and eating has often been viewed as 'a test of moral values,' particularly when it comes to children.[15] Or, perhaps more accurately, when it comes to their mothers. Indeed, the central (albeit often unacknowledged) figure in much commentary on childhood obesity is the 'absent mother.' She can be absent in many ways. Physically absent, because she is in paid employment. Emotionally absent, disengaged from her children's day-to-day activities due to her own fatigue, laziness or ignorance. Morally absent, in that she can't or won't exert discipline in her own house. Absent from the dinner table, a stranger to the stove, missing in action when the fridge or larder is opened by her progeny, distracted or short of time when doing the shopping or preparing the school lunches. If a family is eating too much take-away and processed food, if the kids are overweight, then it's largely the fault of the 'absent mother.'

That much was made clear in the Australian reality show *Honey, We're Killing the Kids*, which screened on Network 10 in 2006. Each episode begins with a profile of a family 'out of control,' a montage of scenes revealing bad eating habits, too much take-away, omnipresent televisions and computers, no exercise, no discipline and little or no home cooking. Enter dietician Dr Anne Purcell and her team of experts, who show the slack parents what their children will look like at forty if their lifestyle habits continue. Standing in a bleak, vault-like room in front of a plasma screen, the parents watch as their beloved offspring age badly, lose their hair and gain huge amounts of weight as the years tick by. On top of that, their haircuts and clothing become unfashionable, their mouths turn down to frowns and scowls and their fore-heads become lined with wrinkles. Their life expectancy is announced to be between five and ten years below the national average. At the end of each digital death sentence, Dr Anne delivers the verdict: 'Mum and Dad – you are killing your kids.'

Over the course of the show, Dr Anne creates a man-ual for each family, with 'simple' rules about cooking and exercise. And certainly, each program shows a significant transformation in each family (at least during the course of filming) from conflict, chaos and hot chips to structure, family togetherness and side salads. A lot seems to be achieved when parents lay down some non-negotiable ground rules, plan ahead and share healthy meals with their kids. But the series reveals a certain gender bias. Dr Anne's guidance and consequent scolding is directed more at the mothers than the fathers. In the first episode, Lauren, the stay-at-home mother of chubby Michaela and Jordan, is lectured about junk food, snacking, and indulging her kids' love for endless episodes of *The Simpsons*. She is encouraged to be a 'better role model' while her husband, Trevor, is largely let off the hook. As Dr Anne hands over the manual of rules for week one, she states: 'This relates to you both but it falls more on you, Lauren.' The same message is delivered the week after: 'A lot is resting on you this week, Lauren,' Dr Anne announces as rules are made for exercise and family time. We see Lauren struggle with her own weight issues, nearly having a panic attack when she ventures into the gym. 'If I really loved my children, I'd sort myself out,' she says mournfully. At the end of the three weeks, changes have been made and Dr Anne is able to share with Lauren and Trevor an alternative vision of their kids' future in which they are healthy, thin, smiling, fashionably dressed and coiffed, destined to live to their late eighties and beyond. And yet despite the TV show's title, much of the one-hour episode is dedicated not to the kids but to their mother. It's all about her inadequacies and her hang-ups.

At least Lauren and her family have the advantage of advantage. Father and husband Trevor has the kind of job that allows his wife to be a full-time carer. The family lives in a large house close to parks and with a big backyard. Other families involved in the show are not so fortunate, particularly those headed by single mothers. One episode focuses on Stormy, a working-class mum with an overweight and demanding daughter, Chenise. The two spend much of the episode crying and fighting. In one painful moment, Stormy breaks down after a particularly virulent clash over second servings of dinner. 'It's the downfall of being on your own. Having to work and raise a child on your own.' But the social critique doesn't last long; it is soon overwhelmed by mother-guilt. Faced with the crystal-ball image of a morbidly obese and depressed forty-year-old Chenise, Stormy observes: 'She's a product of her environment and I am her environment.' There is no father-figure in Chenise's life. Stormy is left to cope solo. In another episode, a single mother of two boys gets some assistance from their father, who has custody every second weekend. She runs a small take-away food business, which means starting work at dawn, finishing at night and relying on the shop's products for family meals. Interestingly, she doesn't slip willingly into the role of scolded child or guilty mother. When Dr Anne gives her the manual of rules for the first week, which includes such edicts as 'cooking meals from scratch,' this single mum asks sarcastically: 'And who will be preparing those?' When Dr Anne praises the children's father for cooking a roast for the kids on his custody weekend, having given Jane the full lecture for feeding the kids take-away kebabs for dinner one evening, Jane is quick to defend herself: 'It's easier if you only have them for a few days.'

The 'absent mother' also features in political discussions about childhood obesity. When Helen Truby met the then federal health minister Tony Abbott at a 2006 conference on obesity in Australia, he told her he was opposed to restricting food advertising to children because he considered it to be the mother's responsibility to regulate kids' food. 'I was infuriated,' Truby told me:

> Governments want to shift the blame onto individuals and say it's their fault. What people need is information about what to do about it. And pressure needs to remain on governments to make structural changes, to pursue policies in terms of availability and affordability of food supply. We need better public transport, better food in schools via tuck shops, more effective treatment strategies we don't have now.

In Truby's view, strategies to combat obesity that depend on shame and guilt have limited usefulness. 'People are fed up with being told they are fat,' she asserted. 'Personally, I don't think that's helpful. If parents are made to feel guilty about their children's weight problems, it makes it very difficult for them to seek help.'

In the last few years, public figures like Tony Abbott have wrangled over how best to combat childhood obesity. In 2004 the then minister for children and youth affairs, Larry Anthony, suggested 'fat camps' as a way to deal with the weight problems of Australian children.[16] Before the 2007 election, the federal Labor Party proposed introducing school-based 'obesity checks' (involving those awful callipers, I bet).[17] The Australian Medical Association has called for bans on soft-drink and chip vending machines in schools.[18] There continues to be intense lobbying for and against a ban on the advertising of junk food to children. A National Obesity Taskforce has been set up to look at these and many other potential strategies. For these public figures and organisations, the topic of childhood overweight and obesity offers more than the chance to chastise negligent mums or wage war against the freedom of corporations to sell lollies to kids. It becomes yet another manifestation of the endless, and perhaps irresolvable, battle about who is responsible for such social problems as addiction, criminality and preventable health conditions – the state or the family. Solutions that don't rely on either censorship or the blame and shame game (such as Jenny O'Dea's suggestion of school or community breakfast programs for children from low socio-economic backgrounds) are rarely discussed.[19] Most experts acknowledge the social gradient to obesity but, as Gard points out, politicians who purport to be deeply concerned about childhood obesity are quick to lecture parents about their responsibilities but 'rarely call for a reduction in poverty.'[20]

*

In August 2006, the hugely successful multicoloured children's entertainment group Hi-5 issued a press release expressing their shock and dismay about childhood obesity having reached 'scary' and 'epidemic proportions.' Instead of pointing the finger at chip and soft-drink manufacturers (sponsors perhaps of their own TV station), the group blamed parents. 'Parents need to be a little bit more strict,' said Hi-5 member Tim Harding. 'Don't give [your children] money to buy a pie at the canteen. Pack healthy lunches. Have a bit more control.' Another member of the group, Charli Delaney, acknowledged that controlling kids' eating habits was hard in the face of the rising costs of healthy food and the long hours worked by parents. She wasn't a mum herself, but she felt Hi-5 was doing its bit by keeping the kids singing and dancing, keeping their minds active, and writing songs about eating vegetables.[21]

I don't want to diminish Hi-5's contribution to the fight against childhood obesity. But urging parents to be less lazy and singing a few songs about carrots is a simplistic approach to a complex issue. But no wonder, if we consider the media's over-hyped and simplistic reporting of the problem and the inadequate and ideological approach of many politicians. The term 'epidemic' conjures up such a woeful vision of the future – hordes of fat kids who can't play sport or who will die before their parents – that we are desperate to identify a single cause and a simple solution. But as Helen Truby told me,

36

one of the difficulties facing parents of overweight and obese children is that there isn't always a simple solution:

> If someone rocks up to their GP and says, 'My child is obese, what do I do?,' well, there are no definitive answers. GPs are in a tricky situation. The usual advice given – eat healthy foods and be more active – doesn't always work for these obese kids. No one really knows the best way to manage them. There is no one thing to blame and there have to be a whole range of strategies to solve it.

I wonder too about the consequences of some of the strategies developed to help children make healthier food choices. For example, a system of colour-coded warning signs for food has been introduced in some primary schools to crack down on anything considered unhealthy.[22] Cake and chips are contraband in some primary schools. 'They sit in a little area and there is a lunch duty teacher and if she sees you eating something like cake or chips, she tells you to put it back and take it home,' one Brisbane mother explained.[23] Often the offending food is wrapped up in red or orange paper, accompanied by a note explaining to the parent why it is not acceptable. I imagine this campaign of lunchbox cleansing might create a new source of social embarrassment for kids. Bringing a cake to school on your birthday to share with your classmates, something that used to happen all the time when I was a kid, is also banned in some schools, not just because of obesity concerns. This is also increasing parental anxiety about other food issues: allergies to nuts, lactose intolerance, gluten intolerance, and fear that additives and preservatives might cause behavioural difficulties. As food academic Nicola Humble points out, modern mothers 'patrol … their children's food and eating with a new intensity.'[24] Concerns about weight are just one of many issues that Australian mums have to cope with, along with all the other stresses and strains associated with feeding a family. Who knows if all this might create new kinds of eating disorders in the future, ones that eclipse our current concerns about obesity and anorexia.

The glaring issue for me in the over-hyped and much-discussed issue of childhood obesity is how we ignore the importance of disadvantage. As the research of Truby and O'Dea shows us, not all children are at risk of becoming obese – it's primarily those from poor backgrounds or those who come from particular ethnic groups. In the context of those groups, the term epidemic may not be an overstatement. If children who have parents of social and economic means do become overweight, they are more likely to seek assistance from health professionals. If we appreciated the role played by economic disadvantage, then espousing 'more parental control' – as has everyone from Hi-5 to government ministers to newspaper columnists – would be exposed for what it is: blaming the poor for their plight.

As I prepared to embark on the next leg of my food tour, I wondered how other forms of disadvantage might affect our day-to-day experiences with food. What do food and cooking reveal about gender and family relations? Is liberation alive in the kitchen? Is the family meal dead? And how do other divisions in our society – ethnic, cultural, geographical – influence how well we eat?

FAMILY DINNERS

Mount Cotton is about forty minutes' drive from the centre of Brisbane. It's quite a way and the taxi driver who picked me up one Thursday night in July seemed mighty pleased about the fare. I had been told Mount Cotton and its surrounds used to be full of market gardens. Travelling towards the evening's destination, I saw that the growing Brisbane suburbs had mostly pushed out the gardens. It was now all largish houses on larger blocks. From the cab window, I only spotted hints of its semi-rural past: a homemade sign advertising fresh eggs and a winery open on the weekends. Arriving at a generously proportioned modern home, I was greeted at the door by a young boy in his school uniform. 'You're here to interview my mum.' It was more a statement than a question. Indeed, I was there to interview his mum Joanna and her neighbour Carla, to find out more about how working women with kids managed the task of family cooking.

Joanna was in the middle of moving and she apologised for the chaos. The doors were open, even on what was a chilly night. Cats and children came and went. The TV provided some muted background noise. We sat at a round table, with tea and some slivers of store-bought chocolate cake. Joanna apologised that she couldn't provide anything home-baked. She was a redhead, with one of those beautifully lined faces, emanating tranquillity. Or was it fatigue? Joanna described herself as 'divorced with three kids.' Her ex lived in the same suburb. Her fourteen-year-old daughter lived with her dad, the youngest son of twelve (my doorman) lived with Joanne, and the eldest, a sixteen-year-old boy, bounced back and forth between the two houses. Joanna worked part-time three days a week in a produce shop doing data entry. Carla, her neighbour, was perkier, more energetic, a fast talker with a sleek black bob. Married with two daughters of seventeen and thirteen, she had been a schoolteacher but now worked part-time doing office admin work.

Although both women worked part-time and had kids of similar ages, it soon emerged that they had very different approaches to family meals. Carla was the menu planner, the self-proclaimed 'fuss pot' who only shopped once a week. 'I tend not to be a packet person. I like to cook from scratch,' she said. Hers was a cosmopolitan repertoire; although she was a supermarket shopper, she would go out of her way to visit particular stores for special ingredients – organic ham, fresh nuts and so forth. Joanna was more of a 'meat and three veg' kind of cook, and not averse to the occasional tinned or frozen meal. 'I am pretty basic but my meals are tasty. You get good at making something if you do it over and over.' For her, cooking involved time she would prefer to spend doing other things. Gone were the meal plans and religious weekly shops of her younger married days. 'I've turned into a convenience shopper, shopping every couple of days, and it's a killer. You spend more, because you always get little extras.'

Divorce had altered the cooking patterns in Joanna's household. She no longer cooked every night. A rigid meal plan seemed increasingly irrelevant. 'Now that they are older, you never know if they are going to be there for dinner or not,' she explained. When she did cook, she did so with minimal fuss. 'If there is only one child here and the others are over at Dad's, we might have something nice and simple like scrambled eggs on toast, like we will have tonight.' Even during my short visit, it seemed Joanna's family life was a relentless juggling act, more so than for her neighbour Carla: three kids, pets, work, moving house, the usual domestic conflicts exacerbated by divorce. She was wistful when I asked her what she would eat when the kids were grown and gone. 'I will have a more substantial lunch and then dinner will be a sandwich!'[1]

Joanna and Carla both shopped locally, at a supermarket fifteen minutes down the road. In the Mount Cotton area, there wasn't much alternative. The only question was when to go to the supermarket (it was best to avoid Thursday mornings and Sunday afternoons, they explained). In terms of price and quality, both recognised the duopoly exercised by Coles and Woolworths, but felt there was little they could do to counter it. What about the cost of food? Had they noticed the drought driving prices up? 'Things are always going up, every week,' said Carla, particularly meat (even mince, the budgeter's friend), fruit and vegetables. Big rains were worse for prices than drought. 'We had a big wet up north recently and zucchinis went up two dollars a kilo,' Carla observed.

On the question of whether it was cheaper to get takeaway or to cook, both were unanimous about the latter. 'If you hunt down some specials, you can put something on the table for two dollars a plate,' said Joanna. While Carla recognised that pizza or burger family meal-deals might be slightly cheaper than the elaborate meals she cooked for her family, there was another price to be paid. 'The big chains offer a cheaper alternative, but not necessarily a healthier one,' she said. Both families indulged in take-away sparingly (maybe two or three times a month), but again there they had different motivations. For Joanna, a trip to McDonald's happened when she was too tired or too busy to cook. For Carla, take-away Thai or fish and chips was a treat for her girls.

What Joanna and Carla did have in common was that both were primarily responsible for family meals. Before kids came along, each had been the main cook in her house, even though they had both worked. Having children hadn't altered this arrangement. Divorce, however, had. When they were married, Joanna's husband, Michael, had cooked occasionally. 'Now, since we've been divorced, he does a lot of cooking.' Since the divorce, Joanna's kids had all learned to cook more. The day before our interview, her eldest son had cooked dinner – chips, sausages and gravy – because Joanna was busy at the new house fixing the floors. In contrast, Carla's kids loved cooking, but only for fun, rather than the daily chore of churning out dinner. If Joanna cooked, her kids had to wash up. Not so in Carla's house; she did the washing up. Why the gender gap in the kitchen? 'I have more time than my husband, even though I do work,' Carla told me. 'We are better at it,' was Joanna's theory. Both seemed on the surface unperturbed by the inequality. Both felt their partners and kids enjoyed their cooking and neither felt taken for granted. However, Carla expressed a few quiet gripes. 'I do reel my husband in to help me when we're entertaining. It isn't just about barbecuing when the guests arrive.' On the topic of day-to-day cooking, there was another little prickle. 'The question I hate most is, "What's for dinner?" That's why I started to menu plan. They ask me, and I say, "Look on the fridge."'

The hour was drawing to a close and I had consumed all my black tea and a few meagre slices of cake. I wanted to talk about the challenges of producing family meals day after day, year in and year out. What did they find difficult about the task? Sitting at the table together wasn't a sticking point. Carla's family 'make a point of eating dinner at the table together, even if it means eating at seven-thirty or eight.' In Joanna's house, at least four dinners a week were eaten together at the table. 'We always try to eat dinner together. Sometimes there are too many people for the table, in which case someone goes over to the TV. We might have the TV on, but we still talk.' The harder task for Joanna was coming up with ideas for family meals. 'My recipe book is pretty lean, pretty basic. It's not really exciting. That's the challenge for me.' Time, for both, was an issue, the management of shopping, planning meals, cooking and cleaning up.

The interview was over. Joanna had deflected every questioning child and ringing phone for the last hour, but I sensed this was becoming increasingly difficult. The doorman was hovering in the kitchen, hopping from foot to foot. He needed his mum. The taxi driver who had driven me to the house arrived to pick me up at seven on the dot. He'd gone to eat dinner in the area and waited until I was done.

'What did you have to eat?' I asked.

'Hungry Jack's,' he said. 'There isn't much else open around here.'

*

43

I spent my second night in Brisbane with another couple of working mums. These women were younger, of my generation: Michelle, thirty, with a seven-year-old son, and Patricia, also thirty, with an eight-year-old son. When I arrived at Michelle's two-storey home in Mansfield, the family was finishing dinner. Dad retired to the TV room, while Mum encouraged her slow-eating boy to finish his serve of chicken and salad. I sat in the dining room in front of tea and biscuits while Michelle, clad in gym gear and sneakers, tried to hurry up her son. 'Why is that lady here?' he wanted to know. Soon Patricia arrived, the son was excused from eating his last piece of lettuce and we started to talk.

I had been told both women worked part-time, but that wasn't exactly the case. Patricia worked three days a week at a bank, but the other two days were spent studying and doing some bookkeeping. Her ultimate goal was to start up her own home-based bookkeeping business. Her current workload sounded more full-time to me. 'It's fairly full on,' she acknowledged. 'As we head towards the end of the financial year the bank wants me to work more, but then the taxes kick in. And I have an eight-year-old. He's a handful.' Michelle's workload was similar. She worked three days a week but was also studying law and criminology as well as looking after her child. Neither could rely on family in the area, although Patricia's brother had recently moved in with them temporarily.

I asked Michelle and Patricia the same questions I had asked Carla and Joanna the previous evening. Both Michelle and Patricia were responsible for grocery shopping, done fortnightly on payday at the local supermarket with top-up trips for milk and bread in between. Husbands could rarely be trusted with the shopping on their own. 'Men tend to buy too much stuff. And they go down the lolly aisle,' Patricia observed wryly. Both tried to avoid going shopping with their sons, who either pestered or complained. Interestingly, Michelle and her husband shared the cooking; no roster involved, just whoever was home first and felt like doing it. Before her son Liam was born, Patricia and her husband had also shared the cooking; now she was responsible. Patricia made a point of telling me that it wasn't as though her husband was relaxing with a beer on the couch while she fried chicken. That's what it was like when she was growing up, one of seven kids, with a stepfather who would come home and watch TV while the girls got dinner ready.

The menu in these two family homes varied. For Michelle, it was mostly meat and vegetables or salad, the occasional curry and regular summer barbecues; 'nothing too exotic,' she explained. 'If I plan out of recipe books, it always makes my weekly shop more expensive. There is always something extra you need to get.' Is she inspired by cooking shows on TV? 'I have seen those shows. I watch them for entertainment rather than content,' she said. The arrival of their son had brought more structure to their meals. 'If it was just us, it might be tinned spaghetti for dinner.' For Patricia, family meals were determined by the health concerns of both son and husband. Her husband's doctor had put him on a low-fat diet, but her son was seriously underweight and required as much fat as possible. So Patricia had to cook three different meals every night. As a consequence, she often relied on pre-prepared foods. 'Food in my family is a major issue, trying to work out how to balance both their needs.'

Both mums had noticed grocery prices rising. For Patricia, whose son was also lactose intolerant, the cost of special products for him was an added burden. Both women believed cooking from scratch ended up cheaper in the long run. Neither relied much on take-away. It was difficult to find time for entertaining, but both families made a point of eating together at the table. Michelle enjoyed cooking, whereas Patricia saw it as a chore. 'I wouldn't say I like it. I don't have a problem doing it.' The barriers to cooking more complicated or varied meals were predictable: too busy, too tired, not interested in meal planning or in spending money on ingredients you'd only use once.

Forty minutes later, I was all out of questions. I did want to know one last thing. Did they feel appreciated for the family meals they produced? There was a bit of a pause. Michelle said she did. Patricia was more equivocal. 'I never really think about it. I suppose so. I've never bothered me that Fred doesn't say thanks for the meal. But now that my brother is living with us, he will actually say thanks for the meal, it was great. My husband will say it now as well.'

Walking away from these encounters, I found myself thinking about the interview effect. Both women were reserved, even shy, about some of the questions I asked. Their answers were often curt and matter-of-fact. Perhaps they thought I was making something out of nothing, expecting to find complexity in what was for them a daily chore that required little analysis. I suppose, too, it's confronting, having to justify your actions, and implicitly your skill as a wife and mother, to a stranger with a tape recorder.

*

According to food historian Margaret Visser, the custom of the family meal dates back two million years 'to the daily return of proto-hominid hunters and foragers to divide food up with their fellows.'[2] While the origins of the family meal might be the clan gnawing prey around a fire, our ideal picture of this daily ritual remains that of a semi-formal gathering around a table, involving both adults and children. As Visser points out, this kind of family meal is an exercise in discipline and togetherness. 'The dining table,' Visser explains, 'is a constraining and control device, a place where children eat under the surveillance of adults' and are 'deliberately encouraged to talk.'[3] In addition, the mark of a 'proper' family meal is one where the TV is turned off.[4] If everyone is spread around the lounge room with their bowls of pasta, eating on couches in front of the TV or PlayStation, children might never learn good manners or the habit of polite conversation. And parents might never learn what's on their kids' minds. Although our notion of a family dining together around a table is quite specific to Western cultures,[5] we still see it as the epitome of good domestic eating, an expression of true family unity. Eating together remains 'the most potent symbol of a happy, secure household.'[6] Consider the following exchange, which I witnessed when I was doing field research for a report on Australian attitudes to family. Four high-school girls, about to face their final-year exams, discussed family dinners:

Girl 1: We all sit down and have dinner together. My dad's big on that. I have to *ask* not to eat with them.
Girl 2: I don't bother asking. I just go.

Girl 3: I can't sit at the dinner table with my mum. I sit in front of the TV. Mum sits at the table.

Girl 4: My family used to always go out on picnics together. Now we hardly see each other. That's when my parents were together.

This wasn't merely a conversation about who eats dinner, when and where. It was about how their respective eating arrangements reflected the closeness, or otherwise, of their families. The underlying, and widespread, assumption is that family dining habits are 'an index of family life.'[7]

No matter how it has changed in recent decades (indeed, perhaps because it has changed so much), the family meal retains much of its symbolic power. The notion of the home-cooked meal, consumed by parents and kids gathered around the table, can still tug the strings of even the most cynical heart. It is a staple of Hollywood films, television advertising and food media. As academic Elspeth Probyn writes, 'the family meal still has an amazing capacity to make us nostalgic for the idea of a simple life, carried by the desire for something that is dependable and unchanging.'[8] We can't help but associate this food with a world we fear is now passing from memory, in which neighbours knew each other, families stayed together and kids roamed the streets with their bikes and their dogs until their mothers called in to dinner.

So potent is the idea of the home-cooked family meal that many commercial foods attempt to harness the concept in their packaging and marketing – particularly those foods we rarely have the time or inclination to make from scratch anymore. We can purchase 'Family Favourite' chicken curry, frozen roast dinners, 'Cook in the Pot' chicken chasseur or sausage casserole. We can buy 'Kitchen Collection' bread mix, ready-made herb bread with the brand name 'La Famiglia,' and 'Home-bake' onion and parmesan bread bearing the slogan 'From our family to yours.' Soup can be made from 'Home-style' split-pea soup mix or, for a quick office snack, there is 'Home-style' pumpkin soup in a cup. For dessert, we are inundated with home-related products: 'Our home-style recipe' triple-chocolate cookies, 'Home-style' raisin and oat cookies, 'Home-made' chocolate-chip cookie dough and any number of offerings from Mrs Fields, Sarah Lee or Nanna. Ready-made foods are labelled with an assortment of phrases associated with the domestic hearth: oven-roasted and oven-baked, traditional, family and chunky. In this way, even the most pathetic, MSG-ridden offering can be 'imbued with the warmth, intimacy, and personal touch' of a home-cooked family meal.[9]

The nutritional superiority of a home-cooked lamb roast with veggies over a frozen roast-lamb dinner is close to indisputable. But some are intent on finding benefits that go beyond the merely nutritional. Joanna Blythman argues that eating together can 'potentially bestow a whole clutch of non-food benefits' such as improved social skills and closer family ties.[10] A 2005 article by obesity researchers in Brisbane found that the odds of being overweight at age fourteen were greater among those whose mothers stated that it was not important that the family ate together.[11] In a summary of American research on family meals, academics Gallup, Syracuse and Oliveri list the numerous social benefits of regular family dinners, including fewer mental health problems and less drug and alcohol abuse.[12] Even celebrity chefs have joined the fray. In an interview for British magazine

Good Housekeeping, Jamie Oliver advocated families cooking and eating together as a sure-fire recipe for domestic bliss. Oliver's interview was to promote one of his latest projects, Home Cooking Day, to encourage British families to eat together on a regular basis:[13]

> What I'd like is to remind families to have a little cook-up and sit round the table regularly. It might sound a bit patronising, but it's not meant to be … I think if you got everyone to eat round the table two or three times a week you'd get a drop in the divorce rate.

Mum is at the heart of Oliver's commentary on the importance of family meals. She is the one liable if family meals are few and far between. He blames the increasing number of working mothers for 'naughty' food choices and the decline of the family dinner:

> As far as holding a family or a nation's food culture together, it's always been women. And when the Industrial Revolution and two world wars kicked in … women went to work and stayed in work … To my mind that's why we've lost our food culture.

Jamie is trying to conjure up a nostalgic view of the family dinner, something that existed in that simple and pure time before the onslaught of second-wave feminism, widespread divorce and the commercialisation of food. This is what Probyn describes as a 'romanticised vision of togetherness that is posed in opposition to a disjointed, fragmented world.'[14]

This romanticised view of the family meal bothers me on two fronts. First, there doesn't appear to be much evidence that family meals are becoming extinct – or indeed that these meals were ever the regular and pleasurable rituals Jamie and others believe them to have been. There have been some well-documented changes in the way families eat. We are eating out more. We are buying more pre-packaged foods.[15] We *may* be eating family meals together only a few times a week rather than every day, and we may be eating those meals on couches in front of the TV rather than at a dinner table. But whether the idyllic world of family meals lauded by Jamie *et al* really existed is hard to say. Despite the odd study here and there, try as I could, I found it difficult to locate any extensive Australian research on the benefits, physical, social or psychological, of family meals. There seemed to be more posturing and educated guesswork.

At the end of 2007, I was employed by food manufacturer Unilever Australia to conduct some research into family mealtimes in Australia.[16] How often do families get together to eat a meal? How important are family meals to parents and children? What are the perceived benefits of family mealtimes? I was excited to be conducting this research because I knew there was little up-to-date Australian data either to support or to counter the perception that the family meal was dying. The research had both qualitative and quantitative aspects, but the most important findings came from a national survey we conducted of over 1000 respondents from all over Australia. The findings proved to be a profound disappointment to anyone searching for evidence that the family meal has been killed off by our modern lifestyle.

Firstly, an overwhelming number of respondents – 93 per cent – reported eating family meals, which we defined as occasions when 'family members gather, at the same time and place, to consume a main meal in the family home.' Seventy-seven per cent reported doing so at least five nights a week. It seems reports of the death of the family meal have been exaggerated. Our survey also revealed that the daily ritual of the family meal is highly valued by Australians, with 86 per cent of respondents reporting that eating family meals together as often as possible was either extremely or very important to them. Women (who – surprise, surprise – were more likely to be the main meal provider)[17] placed more importance on frequent family meals than did men. The perception that people do not care about family meals, and that mothers are the main offenders, thus also proved to be a furphy.

Our research certainly uncovered some interesting findings about the *quality* of the Australian family meal. Generally, family dinners lasted around twenty-five minutes. In 60 per cent of cases, the television was always or often on during dinner, but nearly 60 per cent of all respondents reported eating at the dinner table, rather than in front of the TV. Perhaps the traditional notion of a meal consumed around the table, without electronic distractions, no longer holds. But what was absolutely clear from our research was that the vast majority of Australians still find the time for family meals, value them, and believe they are essential to fostering communication and affection between family members.

I was surprised by the high percentage of respondents who reported eating family meals so frequently. Perhaps this was evidence of over-reporting, a manifestation of parental guilt. Who wants to admit, even to themselves, that they don't make the time to eat with their family regularly? Nevertheless, I was excited about the findings. From the point of view of a media campaign, however, the survey was a dud. Good news is no news. We had just produced some of the most comprehensive research into how families eat, and yet media interest was negligible. Our research didn't support the image of alienated family members slouched on couches in separate rooms, engrossed in sitcoms and video games and eating instant noodles. Instead, the research confirmed what I had suspected when I had interviewed those Brisbane working mothers. Despite all the difficulties they face producing family meals night after night, Australian mothers continue to value and maintain this ritual. 'Good on ya, Mum ...'

*

It pays to be wary of nostalgia. It is hard to see things clearly through misty eyes. As academic Jean Duruz comments, it is easy to be 'beguiled by the sensuality of memories' of home cooking performed by mothers and grandmothers in warm and welcoming kitchens.[18] I remember with deep affection sitting on my *nonna*'s kitchen bench, watching her roll, cut and boil gnocchi, fry pumpkin flowers and crostoli. I have treasured memories of the cakes and slices and tasty dinners that my mother used to prepare in the kitchen of our first home. I know now that this domestic labour, the fruits of which were so enjoyable to me, were bundled up with other, less edifying things – unhappiness, frustration, inequality. Nostalgic thoughts are always selective, dodging the 'political questions of ... whose labour makes this possible.'[19] And so Jamie's evocation of a golden age of family meals, which has been spoiled by the advent of working mothers, ignores an important social fact. Namely that as women have entered the paid workforce in increasing numbers over the past three decades, men haven't taken on substantially more housework to compensate.[20] If Jamie wants to encourage more family meals, why doesn't he criticise those fathers who won't shop, cook and clean for their own families?

Let's turn away from nostalgia and return to reality and the working mothers I visited in Brisbane. All four had a firm commitment to 'cooking from scratch' and didn't seem to rely much on take-away or convenience foods. All were convinced that cooking basic meals was cheaper than using lots of pre-prepared food. That said, I have observed conversations with other mothers who have been at odds on this question. Maybe it would be cheaper to get that Tuesday night pizza deal they spruik during the early edition of the news (buy one pizza and get a second for two dollars). I wanted to test this. Take, for example, a McDonald's 'Value Meal Deal.' For \$7.95 you get a Big Mac, a cheeseburger, a serve of medium fries, a medium Coke and a small sundae. Two of these deals would be enough to feed a family of four, at least if the kids were in primary school. So for sixteen dollars you could quickly sort out a mid-week meal. How much would it cost to cook from scratch an equivalent meal if you shopped at the local supermarket (minus the cost of tomato sauce, pickles, ice-cream topping and other bits and pieces)?

Four sesame seed rolls	\$2.20
Six cheese slices	\$2.10

Six frozen hamburger patties	$1.40
One large brown onion	26 cents
Half an iceberg lettuce	$2.20
1.25 litre Coke	$1.65
Half a kilo of fries	$1.35
500 grams of vanilla ice-cream	$1.70
Total	$12.86

That's a saving of only around three dollars if you make your own Value Meal Deal. But what about the other incidental expenses? The time-cost of driving to and from the local McDonald's: anywhere between ten and thirty minutes. The time-cost of ordering and waiting for your food: ten minutes. Compare this with the time-cost of shopping, preparing and cleaning up after a homemade Value Meal Deal: anywhere between two and three hours. The cost of not having to cook when you are tired, plus the kids' excitement about eating at McDonald's? Priceless. But the mothers I spoke to recognised that there is another cost involved in all this, a serious long-term cost to their family's health. It's a mark of their dedication as parents that they persevere with the daily chore of cooking.

The issue of time is crucial here. While Joanna, Michelle and the other women I met didn't seem to find it difficult to make time to eat together, other families may well struggle to do so, having to accommodate different work and school schedules, with parents working overtime or shiftwork, kids with casual jobs and extracurricular activities, not to mention different eating habits and preferences. As Visser comments, it's a wonder that busy parents go on staging family meals at all. They continue to do so, perhaps because they feel their kids need these meals, and because 'dinner-table conversation becomes a unique opportunity for the family to find out what all its members are thinking and doing.'[21] Joanna and Michelle had the time to shop and prepare very basic meals. Carla had the time and the desire to experiment with the more exotic. And Patricia, who had to prepare three different meals every day, relied more on pre-prepared foods. But all had basic cooking skills, learnt from mothers and home-economics teachers rather than from cooking shows and foodie media.

Whether or not you possess any basic cooking skills can have a huge impact on what you choose to eat. In writing about the effect of 'the harried environment' on people's weight, academics Broom and Strazdins make the important point that cooking skills (or lack of them) can often influence attitudes to food preparation time. 'Going for fast food takes as long as making a salad sandwich, but ... people may not perceive it that way, especially if they have little experience with basic food preparation.'[22] Without basic skills, cooking is much more time-consuming. An omelette can take an hour instead of twenty minutes. It may be quicker to order a stir-fry from the local Thai establishment than to whip one up yourself. As home-economics teacher Janet Caincross explained to me, many of the students she encounters in the early years of high school have little or no experience with cooking implements, hardly any idea about how to read a recipe and a limited repertoire of ingredients. Almost all of their cooking experience is with prepared or partially pre-pared foods. 'They prepare their own meals or meals for the family because their parents are working late. They will pre-pare what's quick and easy. Pasta with sauce from a jar. Pizza muffins.' The time it takes to make a pasta sauce from scratch may seem onerous if you are struggling with peeling the garlic or slicing the onions. But even the skilful, starved of time, have difficulties. Standing at the school gates after our interview, Janet confessed that she often worked until seven at night, leaving her too tired to cook. 'I get take-away or I call my parents and say, "What are you eating and can I have some?"'

*

In May 2006, the Danish royal chef of twenty-four years, Takashi Kondo, quit his job in disgust at what he described as the Danish royal family's preference for microwave dinners and reheated leftovers instead of gourmet meals. He blamed this shift in the monarchs' eating habits on labour efficiency and time constraints. 'Everyone has to run around and hurry everything,' were Kondo's departing words as he slammed the door of the royal kitchen.[23] It seems even families with domestic staff and limitless resources struggle to make time for family dinners.

In the hearts and minds of professional foodies and home economics teachers, there is a special dining room in hell reserved for 'convenience foods.' For Michael Symons, 'convenience foods' are 'another nail in the coffin of the family meal,' and 'functional foods' are 'among numerous other indicators of the continuing decline of domestic eating.'[24] This is an overstatement. While families, for different reasons, might have to rely on pre-prepared and take-away foods to help them get through the week, there is still plenty of evidence that the family meal is not extinct. Indeed, this was one of the more sensible conclusions from the research by Gallup *et al.* Despite numerous barriers, people still managed to eat half their weekly meals with their families (more importantly, they said they wanted to eat with their families more often).[25] Given the various pressures on families, it is quite an achievement that many still bother.

Perhaps, of course, today's mums don't bother quite as much as their predecessors did, opting instead to prepare straightforward, tasty fodder. Academic Jane Baxter argues that while Australian working women are still primarily responsible for family meals, they are preparing less elaborate meals. It used to be that the skill of a domestic cook was measured by what she could do with scant resources – meat loaf, tuna mornay, spag bog, stews and soups are all dishes designed to stretch ingredients to feed a family on a budget. This need still exists for many, but the more scant resource nowadays is time. The new style of family meals is built around that principle. Meals planned, prepared and cooked with a minimum of fuss, to fit competing schedules, in that slim window of opportunity between coming home from work and the posing of that annoying question, 'What's for dinner?' A return to some idealised past of Sunday roasts and a constant stream of complicated dishes served up on a daily basis around the communal table is neither possible nor preferable if current household inequalities remain. Until some parity is reached, what does it matter if Mum has to 'cheat' sometimes? While the foodies might sneer, a jar of pasta sauce or a store-bought roast chicken is a small price to pay in order to get dinner on the table and all the family members around it.

SEX IN THE KITCHEN

I arrived early for the first class of He Cooks, a cooking course designed for men who, according to the brochure, 'want more confidence in the domestic kitchen.' The classroom looked like it had been built for high-school home economics; indeed, the community college was once a local public school. A trestle table was set austerely in an adjoining room. Two young men prepared tools and ingredients for the night's activities. Both had the lean and hungry look of men who have spent hours on their feet in commercial kitchens. Soon the owner of He Cooks, Ben Dalton, arrived with an armful of baguettes and pide. Ben started He Cooks in 2003 and now runs classes in Sydney and Melbourne. 'It's a pity you can't see our students in their natural habitat,' he said to me. 'With a woman around, they show off and make jokes. Or they get defensive.'

Soon after Ben disappeared into the kitchen, the first student arrived, a softly spoken man in his fifties, 'Tim.' This cooking course was a gift from his 28-year-old daughter, who thought it was about time he learned how to cook. Since his wife passed away, Tim had been living on take-away, barbecued chops and meals at the leagues club. His wife had been the family cook, even though she'd had a paid job. Tim never learnt the basics. Now he was keen to try. He told me that when he did get the chance to make 'a special meal,' he enjoyed it. What was the last special meal he had cooked? Well, just last week he'd made Atlantic salmon, mashed potatoes and veggies for 'a lady friend.'

Tim and I were then joined by two other students, both of them divorced. There was 'Marlon,' a towering, broad-shouldered sixty-year-old, a gourmand who had just returned from a motorcycle tour of Europe. All his life, Marlon had never learnt how to cook. He had always been catered for, moving from family home to boarding school to university to married life. His wife had been in the restaurant business so, during their thirty-five years of marriage, either she cooked for him or he ate in the restaurant. Newly separated and living in an area of Sydney well stocked with chef-hatted restaurants, he had been well fed by Neil Perry and the like. But now it was time to learn how to, in his words, 'look after myself.' The other student was younger, only forty; the ink on his divorce papers was still fresh. The inspiration to cook, he told me, first came from flicking through those foodie magazines at the dentist's office and thinking 'that looks great, wouldn't it be great to be able to make that?' 'I'm doing this not to learn how to cook to survive but to cook to entertain.' When they were together, his ex-wife had done the cooking. Now, when he had custody visits with his two daughters, they tended to eat out.

Along with these newly single men there was also a married man, a 34-year-old father of one, 'Nelson.' Tall and trim, he had been trying to do the He Cooks course since it started, but every time he had planned to enrol, work commitments intervened. His wife, who is a stay-at-home mum, was the household cook. 'I come from South Africa, where I was spoilt by my mum, spoilt by the lifestyle. I know how to make peanut butter on toast. That took a few tries, though. I have three options at the moment when it comes to food: my wife cooks, I eat take-out or I go hungry.' Nelson was eager to learn how to make something other than quick breakfast fare. 'I won't have to go hungry if my wife's angry with me,' he joked. But he also recognised that cooking could be both relaxing and creative.

Soon the class was called into the kitchen by the instructor chef, Cas. Beers in hand, looking tentative, they crowded around the bench-top at the front of the class. Cas was the perfect teacher for this crowd. Laid back and clearly heterosexual, he had the aura of a man who could deal with an oil fire while speedily chopping up spring onions. Cas had worked in notable restaurants such as Balzac and Pier, with a long stint at David Thompson's Michelin-starred restaurant in London. Tired of the long hours, hard work and uncertain rewards of the commercial kitchen, he retired and began training as a carpenter, working for He Cooks on the side. After a few health and safety tips ('If we have to evacuate due to fire, we'll head down the stairs and towards the pub,' said Cas), the class got straight into learning how to prepare a warm chocolate tart. The tart seemed a daunting task, but Cas reassured them. 'If you are sleeping on the couch, this tart is the best way to get back into the bedroom.' Cas gave them tips on buying pastry cases from the supermarket. No knowledge is assumed at He Cooks, and that was just as well, judging by the apprehensive looks on the students' faces. Cas popped the tarts in the oven. 'See, it's that easy,' he said. 'Looks easy,' mumbled Marlon as he took a swig of his beer.

We then moved on to making pesto from scratch for a pasta entrée. I watched as the youngest member of the class, a 22-year-old uni student, dipped slices of baguette into oil and balsamic vinegar. 'Elvis' had long hair, horn-rimmed glasses and an earring. When I interviewed him at the start of the class, he displayed a nervous intelligence. He had been considering doing the course for some time. As an only child of European parents, all he knew how to cook was an omelette. His mother's proficiency in the kitchen had been a barrier to his learning. 'Every time I watch Mum cook, I think, I can't do that!' His father was lord of the barbecue and a former army cook, but his mother was the family food provider. Elvis had recently shed twenty-two kilograms and wanted to learn to cook for health reasons, but also for cultural ones. 'Amongst my friends, I'm the culture person,' he told me with some pride. And so it made sense to him that he should know about food. What about his male friends – were they foodies? 'I have male friends who know how to cook but I have a lot more male friends who need to learn,' Elvis said.

Once the pesto had been stirred into a pot of steaming pasta, it was served up to the students and we sat down to eat. 'Not first-class cooking, but much better than the Maggi noodles or some of the other stuff you guys would reach for in the pantry,' was Cas's verdict. The talk over pasta was about how the Australian food scene had changed over the years, evolving from the odd Chinese restaurant and hamburger joint to a wide variety of ethnic restaurants, as well as the arrival of fast food. Tim talked about his childhood, when it was only chops and three veg for dinner and the regular Sunday roast, a time when chicken was a rare dish.

'Now there is so much to choose from,' he said with approval.

Pasta polished off, we returned to the kitchen with a fresh set of beers to tackle the hands-on aspect of the course: Atlantic salmon fillets on an avocado and apple salad. Cas prepared the dish first, and then the men got down to work. As I sampled Cas's example, he and I talked, watching the men as they grated and chopped, referring back to the recipe every few seconds. Cas told me that for most of his students, this course was a gift from a girlfriend or wife, a not-so-subtle hint. For others, the urge to enrol had been sparked by a divorce or the death of a partner. 'Now, they are fighting for themselves,' he told me. The students ranged from teens to seniors, although their backgrounds were generally similar, mostly men with money, sophistication and social capital. Cas reckoned TV shows and celebrity chefs had made cooking more popular with everyone, including men. 'Now chefs are on the red carpet,' he said with a smile.

Cas rushed off to rescue Tim, who was struggling to flip over his salmon fillet. 'You have to treat it like a woman,' Cas instructed, as he tenderly slipped the spatula under the fish and turned it on its side. Tim glanced furtively in my direction. Was he embarrassed for himself or on my behalf? It wasn't clear to me, and I looked away; I went back to scribbling in my notebook. As they all 'plated up,' they chatted about the Swans' chances in the finals. I walked over to inspect Tim's dish. 'Your daughter will love that when you make it for her,' I said to him. 'Does the wife know you are taking this class?' Elvis asked Tim. Tim stared at the fish for what felt like ten minutes, although it must have been only ten seconds. 'She died. That's why I'm doing this course,' was the eventual response. Elvis apologised profusely, but I reflected that Tim must now be used to this – to strangers asking hurtful questions unintentionally. As the men folded up their latex aprons, they seemed pleased with themselves, having prepared something both presentable and edible without loss of limb or explosion. Nelson looked over in my direction. 'I don't know what you women go on about – this is easy!'

As I sat and watched them eat, I finally got the chance to corner the only member of the class I hadn't yet spoken to, a forty-year-old father of two, 'David.' This course was neither part of divorce therapy nor a gift from a female relative; he was here at the urging of his eight-year-old son, who was mad about cooking. 'He wants to be either an artist or a chef – he's very creative,' David told me. This cheerful father had tried to wriggle out of this evening's lesson but his son wouldn't hear of it. 'I called him and said I was thinking about skipping it due to work but he wouldn't let me.' In their household of two kids, David barbecued but his wife was the cook. 'She hates the daily routine cooking but she likes to entertain.' What did she think about this course? 'She would love me to cook more often.' After the night's experience, he was now contemplating taking one of the father and son classes that He Cooks runs.

Ben, the founder and owner of He Cooks, explained that the impetus for starting the school had been his own lack of cooking skills. 'Twelve years ago I woke up and realised I couldn't cook more than three things. I would just keep cooking the same thing every time it was my turn to cook.' Wanting to learn but unimpressed by the courses on offer, he came up with the idea of a guys-only, hands-on cooking school. 'Men like to learn by doing so we get them straight into it.' Ben emphasised that the students come from diverse backgrounds. 'One course we had a seventeen-year-old about to go overseas on a cricket scholarship; his mum bought him the course so he would know how to look after himself. We also had a seventy-year-old ex-diplomat whose wife was terminally ill and he had to look after both her and him for the first time ever.' Ben believed that food had become a new interest for men. 'Since I've started the cooking school, I'm having conversations with guys about food now, whereas normally it would have been sport or politics. These days, food is a much more unifying or shared topic of conversation for guys.' I talked to him about Tim, how learning to cook may well be an important, practical step in the grieving process. It was quite moving that these men, whether prompted by hardship or love, were prepared to overcome their lack of confidence in the kitchen. 'That's right,' Ben said. 'In that sense, it's both powerful and liberating.'

I left these powerful and liberated men to wash the dishes and eat their warm chocolate tart. I thanked them all for their time, promised them anonymity in the book, and disappeared out the door, wishing I could have left a tape-recorder on the table to catch their woman-free talk.

*

I went to He Cooks in an attempt to understand why men cook; or, more accurately, why they don't.[1] Certainly this was a select group – men who can't cook but are bothered enough to learn. But my experience at He Cooks confirmed what I already suspected. Whether working or not, enthusiastic gourmets or not, women tend to take charge of the family cooking. Men barbecue.[2] When women aren't around, men rely on restaurants or take-away. Any desire among men to learn how to cook is prompted by a basic concern for survival, to woo or to entertain. There was no talk about needing a store of recipes to cater for a fussy partner or for lactose-intolerant children. On the other hand, it was clear that younger generations of men – 22-year-old Elvis and the sons of the older He Cooks students – were interested in food and cooking. Both Ben and Cas believed cooking was now cool for guys, thanks to the efforts of celebrity chefs like Jamie Oliver. Was this an indication of a generational shift?

There has always been a gender gap in the kitchen. While the domestic kitchen has been female-dominated, the industrial kitchen has mostly been the sphere of men. There is, in fact, a lot of macho chest-thumping associated with cooking as a profession. This works to entrench the idea that men are the sex best equipped for the tough task of wielding the frying pan in a real restaurant. In his portrait of the Michelin-star-struck restaurant scene in France, Rudolph Chelminski describes the professional kitchen as 'a competitive, unforgiving man's world' and likens the chefs to an army battalion, a rugby team and a gang.[3] Anthony Bourdain uses similar language in his bestselling and hugely entertaining memoir *Kitchen Confidential*. Bourdain recognises that his book is 'obnoxious and overtestosteroned.'[4] Yet such an acknowledgement does little to counter his endless descriptions of the grizzled, scarred, cutthroat, 'thuggish and heavily tattooed,' 'hardcore, ass-kicking, name-taking' cooks who inhabit his kitchen. The kitchen is like a battle zone, with the chef as General Patton and the staff as his troops.

In his essay collection, *The Nasty Bits*, Bourdain describes dinner service in a busy restaurant kitchen in exactly these terms:

> At times like these, under fire, in battlefield conditions, the kitchen reverts to what it has always been since Escoffier's time: a brigade, a paramilitary unit … Move forward … Take that hill!'[5]

In this evocation of the restaurant kitchen as a cross between *Gangs of New York* and *The Green Berets*, the female reader comes away with an unshakeable sense that she is in inhospitable terrain. Of course, Bourdain is right – a restaurant kitchen in full swing is a dangerous place, where only the mad, bad and well co-ordinated survive. But despite Bourdain's occasional efforts to point out that some women are just as capable as men of surviving in this environment, the effect is to reinforce the notion that men are the serious cooks and women are the meatloaf makers.

Some celebrity chefs are more explicit in their view that women can't be serious cooks. In 2005, footballer turned celebrity chef Gordon Ramsay mouthed off about young women in the kitchen:

> They can't cook to save their lives. When they eat, they cheat. It's ready meals and pre-prepared meals all the way … There are huge numbers of young women out there who know how to mix cocktails but can't cook to save their lives, whereas men are finding their way into the kitchen in ever growing numbers.[6]

This is the same guy who declared that women are ineffective in the kitchen when they are menstruating. At least women might have a biological reason for their temper tantrums. What's Ramsay's excuse?[7]

Such attitudes might go some way towards explaining why women are under-represented in the top levels of our commercial kitchens. While women make up 58 per cent of the catering industry workforce, they make up only 23 per cent of head chefs.[8] He Cooks teacher Cas told me that in his time in the industry he had seen many women make great headway in their careers as chefs, only to drop out after a few years. 'It's such a physically demanding job; you are crammed in this room with ten sweaty guys all day.' Women may also be leaving these demanding jobs in the kitchen for the same reasons they leave other male-dominated professions with crippling hours – family commitments. What an irony that women stop cooking in restaurants in order to boil eggs back home.

Once we leave the commercial kitchen, we see the gender roles reversed. In the domestic kitchen men have generally been regarded as hopeless when it comes to food, a nuisance at the chopping board, unreliable and undiscerning shoppers and often unreasonably conservative in their food tastes. Their main role has been to dictate the menu. As food historian Barbara Santich explains, traditionally 'the wage-earning male' was 'offered larger servings or allowed additional foods.' His preferences often determined the family menu (*Where's the meat? None of that wog food for me!*).[9]

But what of Cas and Ben's assertions about the growing numbers of men interested in cooking? There are certainly anecdotal indications that cooking without the aid of a barbecue is no longer considered effete. Some people put that down to the increasing number of blokey celebrity chefs: Jamie Oliver, his mates Ben O'Donoghue and Curtis Stone, as well as Neil Perry, Peter Evans, Matt Moran, Bill Granger and Tobie Putock.[10] There are also more cookbooks aimed at men on the market. The head of programming for the Lifestyle Channel has claimed that men constitute half the audience for their prime-time cooking shows.[11] This is food media for the new bloke, a guy who loves his beer and his football but is sophisticated enough to navigate his way around the kitchen, to appreciate food beyond the drive-through and the microwave.

Despite all this evidence, I am still left with questions. While men might be more interested in food, are they actually cooking more? And if so, what kind of cooking are they doing?

If you look closely at the 'new bloke' or 'new lad' cooking shows and publications, it is clear that cooking is predominantly positioned as a form of leisure, rather than as domestic labour.[12] The emphasis is on fun, entertainment, feeding yourself and your mates and having a laugh, rather than on the drudgery of everyday cooking, which might include satisfying an unappreciative partner or fickle and demanding kids.[13] In Jamie's kitchen, at least in the early incarnation of his TV show, cooking is something he does to entertain his friends or cater for his garage band, before he goes surfing or takes a trip to the dogs. This emphasis on fun is pivotal to the success of these 'blokes in the kitchen' shows. We don't want cooking to seem like a chore. Ben O'Donoghue and Curtis Stone are a case in point. In the third series of their popular ABC program *Surfing the Menu*, their cooking exploits are presented as part sporting contest, part boy's-own adventure:

> Bender and Curtis will compete with each other throughout this series; to catch the biggest fish or the tallest wave, bake the richest cake, take the longest downhill run, create the tastiest entrée, swim with the biggest whale, and in the case of single Curtis, maybe even win the hand of a fair maiden ...[14]

On one level, Jamie and his mates are creating a modern version of 'the bachelor kitchen.' 'The bachelor kitchen' exists in harmony with the female-dominated domestic kitchen; it in no way undermines the central role of wife and mother as food provider. For the playboy bachelor, cooking is a choice, not an obligation, a leisurely pursuit and a cultural activity rather than a household chore. According to academic Joanna Hollows, *Playboy* food and wine columns of the 1950s and 1960s presented cooking as a masculine activity if it involved meat, alcohol, the outdoors, spicy food and food with which to seduce the dupable female.[15] Gastronomic foreplay, in short.

Today's bachelor kitchen is not untouched by feminism. Both Jamie Oliver and Bill Granger grapple with family cooking and cooking for kids. Granger in particular projects an image of a competent dad in the kitchen, serving up every-day meals to his wife and kids with his phosphorescent smile and un-besmirched white T-shirt. Ian 'Hewy' Hewitson is another example, albeit one who appeals more to the mature cook; his dishes are primarily everyday fodder for the busy family. But despite this, cooking shows reinforce more than they refigure traditional gender roles.[16] Indeed there is ample evidence that men and women cook differently: different meals at different times for different reasons. Men's cooking is presented as 'cause for applause,'[17] while women are still doing the everyday cooking.

Here's an example. One Tuesday, passing time over coffee at my local eatery, I picked up Good Living, the *Sydney Morning Herald*'s weekly food supplement. It includes a regular column entitled 'Homecook Hero,' in which readers nominate someone, friend or family member, who is a whiz in the kitchen. This particular week it was Richard, a 55-year-old father of two adult children. Because Richard works lawyer hours, he spends little time in the kitchen during the week; weekend fare is his domain. Healthy, easy food is his preference and he's the cook when it's time to entertain. There is talk of a wife, who cooks during the week, but the article is silent about what she cooks or whether she works.[18] So Richard's cooking is on show for guests, a leisure activity for the weekend. His cooking gets the props while his wife's midweek cooking keeps the family going day to day.

For women, whether in paid work or not, this day-to-day cooking is just one of their home-front duties. Indeed, all the research into the division of unpaid labour shows women are still primarily responsible for household tasks in the average Australian home. Housework consumes almost one third of women's waking hours, compared with one fifth of men's. It's important to note that this inequality applies regardless of levels of paid work. Even if both partners work full-time, women still do more household chores.[19] But what about food preparation and clean-up in particular? In 2006, men spent twenty-eight minutes a day on these tasks. Women spent twice as much time: one hour and eight minutes per day. Eighty-four per cent of all women were involved in food-related chores, compared with 60 per cent of men. What about partners who work similar hours in paid employment? Still the inequality exists, with men spending significantly less time on food preparation than women.[20]

Those apron strings are hard to untie. The connection between women and domestic cooking is strong. Academic Susan Sheridan reminds us that 'lady' derives from the Old English word for 'bread-kneader.'[21] Men are the bread-winners and women the bread-makers. Despite the advent of feminism and the influx of women into paid work, women are still seen to bear the primary responsibility for food preparation in the home. Food media continues to reflect this. Early food TV was aimed squarely at housewives, and early TV chefs like Delia Smith in the United Kingdom, Julia Child in the United States, and Margaret Fulton and Charmaine Solomon in Australia all looked and sounded just like Mum. Their televised lessons showed attentive homemakers how to prepare proper meals for their families.[22] In some respects, more contemporary celebrity chefs like Stephanie Alexander and Maggie Beer are also in this vein. The ultimate example of this is Nigella Lawson. Everything about her persona – from the way she chops an onion to the way her TV shows and books emphasise the joys of simple home cooking – ensures she could never be mistaken for a 'real chef' of the Gordon Ramsay variety.

This close association between women and domestic cooking has created a double bind. For many women, cooking is a way of showing that they are feminine and caring.[23] It cements their place at the heart of the family. A 1987

Mackay Report on food found that 'when it comes to food, Mum is still omnipotent and omniscient.' And not much has shifted in two decades. Mum is still the one responsible for the health and nutrition of the family, despite time constraints and work pressures. In fact, the act of cooking can become particularly important to the working mum struggling to keep her life in balance. It is a symbol, amidst the frenetic pace of it all, that she can still do the right thing by her family. See, I can run a small public relations firm and still make brownies! Cookies to assuage guilt for not being a good mother? It's a new kind of comfort food.

*

We are all exposed to the idea that food is an expression of feminine love throughout childhood. It was re-enforced in a particularly pointed way by my high school home-economics teacher, Ms Starling. In our first class with her we learnt how to bake a cake from scratch: the full deal, creaming the butter and sugar together, sifting the flour and using good quality vanilla essence. The class was only seventy minutes long, so it was a genuine rush to get the mixture finished and into the oven in time to clean up the inevitable mess. I recall stuffing hot slices of cake into my mouth as I rushed to a double period of French.

The next week, Ms Starling presented us with a packet mix, again a vanilla cake. No reading a complicated recipe – just water and an egg, a quick whiz with the electric mixer and into the oven. Enough time for cooking, cleaning up and gossip around the table about the goings on at recess. Just before the end of class, Ms Starling cleared her throat to deliver the punchline. 'Now girls, you have made a cake from scratch and one from a packet mix. Which one did you think was better?' Like all keen schoolgirls, we were eager to tell our teacher what she wanted to hear. But I had no idea what to say. They were both pretty tasty; different textures for sure, but I took an entirely democratic approach to cake at the time. One of my fellow classmates finally took the plunge. 'The cake made from scratch?' she offered. Ms Starling smirked. 'Yes, Fiona, the cake made from scratch. Anything made from scratch is always better than the cheating version. Food is all about caring for others. So remember: if you love your family, you will always go to the extra trouble to make something without any help from Mr White Wings.'

Even at thirteen, I knew this was rubbish. My mum made cakes from scratch and also from packet mixes. Her chosen mode of baking depended entirely on whether she was going through a busy week at work. She was a full-time teacher with two kids and a husband who couldn't have boiled an egg if Paul Bocuse had held a gun to his head. She loved us, regardless of what was baking in the oven. As Tina Turner might have put it, what's packet mix got to do with it? But for women, the idea that cooking for your family is a reflection of your competence as a mother is as ingrained as beetroot juice on a business shirt.

Of course, in this clash of guilt, obligation, stress and the unequal distribution of household responsibilities, resentment is a natural consequence. And so it isn't surprising that some women have come to hate the day-to-day grind of feeding their families, particularly if their family is demanding, fussy or unappreciative. In her 1990 study of forty-nine women living in a low-income Adelaide suburb,

Barbara Santich found that around 35 per cent of those she interviewed disliked cooking, a finding consistent with a number of similar overseas studies. The reasons cited included time limitations, the constant need to think up new dishes, and the need to accommodate the preferences of husband and children. These women saw cooking as an inevitable chore that took up time they would rather spend doing other things. They were particularly averse to the task if they had a partner who found fault with their cooking. Interestingly, these reluctant cooks did not try to shift their cooking responsibilities to other members of the household, suggesting that they accepted, albeit grudgingly, their role as the family food provider.[24]

*

But what of the current generation of boys, who have grown up during the explosion of food media and the rise of the blokey celebrity chef? Has this had an impact on their interest in cooking? Some fathers seem to think so. In a newspaper column, father of two Ian Matthews writes about his cooking enthusiast son, a teenager who hides copies of *Gourmet Traveller* under his mattress and 'experiments' with rosemary and garlic. Matthews writes:

> The main problem these days is that cooking has suddenly become cool. And there has also been some role reversal over the past few years. It always used to be girls in the kitchen and boys in the shed. But compared to my daughter, who can't boil water, my son has become a kitchen freak.

Of course, Matthews sees the kitchen as an overtly masculine domain, with lots of 'sharp steel,' 'naked flames,' 'dead animals' and 'Nigella Lawson to clear up all the mess.'[25] Matthews' son aside, recent research illustrates that we are far from achieving gender parity. Academic Barbara Pocock has found that many Australian boys still cling to the belief that their future wives will do the majority of the housework, including food preparation. While some boys expect to help out, Pocock found that few envisaged a 50:50 split.[26] My hopes for an army of enthusiastic male cooks diminishes in the light of these research findings.

In pursuit of hope, I went to interview a teacher who has spent over fifteen years teaching cooking in co-ed schools, both state and independent. I met Janet Caincross at her current place of employment, a modest Catholic high school in an equally modest western suburb of Sydney. The school population mirrors the population in the surrounding suburbs – working- and middle-class kids from a variety of cultural backgrounds: Portuguese, Islander, Vietnamese and Chinese. Janet was trained as a home-economics teacher but had to re-train after her discipline was remodelled. She now teaches food technology to students from Years 7 to 12, as well as a vocational education course in hospitality.

What I really wanted to know was whether, over the last decade or so, Janet had seen a rising interest among boys in cooking. I was pleased to find out that yes, she had noticed a shift. 'When I first started teaching food tech in a co-ed school, I would only have a handful of boys. In my last two classes at this school, boys have made up half the class. It has improved. When they are looking at it as a career path, it would be close to equal numbers.' In the Year 10 elective food class she was teaching when we met she had 'a good mix of boys and girls from different backgrounds, from the kids with ADHD to the smartest kids in the year group.'

Janet had no illusions; she knew that her students, male and female, were not initially attracted to her classes because they wanted to refine their recipe for mushroom risotto. 'They choose this subject because they think it will be a bludge. And because they like the eating side of it,' she explained. Finding out that the class requires both work and skill can often come as a rude shock to her students. Nevertheless, many of the boys continue with the subject because it is accessible and can lead to employment opportunities. Are they encouraged by celebrity chefs like Jamie Oliver? 'They are,' Janet told me. 'Good male role models like Jamie are important. They like his down-to-earth style. There has been a change in advertising, too. It's not always women who are portrayed in the kitchen. You see men as well.' Are the boys who take on cooking subjected to any kind of teasing? Janet didn't think so. 'There definitely isn't the same stigma as there used to be. That was one of the key reasons why home economics was remodelled. For over ten years, it has been a technology subject.' And so cooking has become more attractive to boys by shaking off its house-wifey associations and becoming 'technological' and 'vocational,' a skill rather than a chore.

After our chat in the staffroom, Janet took me through the two classrooms where she teaches. The first was for those in the junior years, who make scones and muffin pizzas. It looked very much like the home-economics classrooms I remember from my school days: a horseshoe of white linoleum and electric stoves, walls covered with collages about food groups and safety rules. Images of Jamie Oliver decorated the walls, alongside the obligatory Jesus on the cross. Next door was the industrial kitchen used by students undertaking the certificate in hospitality: it was all well-worn stainless steel, big ovens with gas burners, rows of knife rolls and jumbo kitchen utensils. As we left this second classroom, Janet told me about a friend of hers who worked at a Catholic girls' school in the outer western suburbs. 'Her school and their all-boys equivalent recently went through a refurbishment. The girls' school wanted a more conventional domestic kitchen, whereas the boys' school wanted the commercial kitchen.' His and hers kitchens. Not exactly the evidence of a generational shift I was looking for.

*

My mother hates to cook. This is despite the fact that when I was a child, her cooking was excellent. Year after year, she turned out tasty midweek dinners and impressive dinner-party fare. I remember a handful of times when my father cooked, episodes in which he used every pot and dish in the house and required endless streams of praise for his efforts. He did, naturally, barbecue. Perhaps if Mum had installed a skylight above the stove, he would have been happy to cook a steak inside from time to time. It was only after my parents separated that her true feelings about cooking were made known. Made known by the speed at which she dropped the practice and familiarised us with the phone numbers of various pizza delivery places. My sister and I took up cooking fairly quickly – and we both love cooking today.

I think my mum's dislike of cooking stems from the experience of her mother, my *nonna*. Nonna was a brilliant cook. Like most Italians without means, she left school early to

78

work for her family. Her chief role was childminder and cook for the extended Bellini brood and the men who worked her father's farm in northern Queensland. Once married, she cooked for a reticent and unappreciative husband. He would have been happy with a slice of cheese and a crust of bread for dinner, but Nonna kept cooking all the traditional dishes: *gnocchi con sugo*, *polpette*, *melanzane alla parmigiana* and *zuppa inglese*. She collected recipes. She was always interested in what I was cooking. She loved how cooking for her family made her feel: loved and needed.

Cooking as a time-consuming chore, evidence of the oppression of women? Or cooking as an expression of love, as creativity, as culture and an essential life-skill? Both strains are there in my own family history. To my mother's bemusement, I have taken Nonna's path and continue to love cooking on a daily basis. I might be considered a 'domestic feminist,' one of those women who see traditional women's skills and crafts, such as sewing, knitting and baking, as an affirmation of their independence. 'Domestic feminism,' according to its enthusiasts, makes women more independent and self-sufficient, less reliant on corporations and outsourcing. As academic Elspeth Probyn writes, 'Beyond the now tattered dream of liberation in the bedroom, and freed from the obligations of cooking, the kitchen is now sold to women as the new sphere of sensual liberation.'[27] But I fear the desire to refigure cooking as liberating reveals the unease we feel about it as feminists. We know cooking has a gendered history and continues to reflect gender inequality. These are things we can't easily ignore.

Sometimes I wonder if women have to shoulder some of the responsibility for their own status as the designated household cooks. Are we too impatient with the men in our lives when they attempt to learn how to cook? Do we shove them aside too readily and say, 'That's not how you chop an onion?' Of course, a popular male trick when asked to perform household labour is to do it so badly and so slowly that they are never asked to do it again. But there is something to be said for creating the space, time and opportunity for men to learn, even if it means eating dinner at 10 p.m. until they get the hang of it. Or perhaps women should heed Jamie Oliver's recent suggestion that they deny their men sex until men start pulling their weight in the kitchen.[28]

There is a glimmer of hope in the next generation of boys, thanks in part to the revamp of home economics into a technical subject and the role-modelling provided by Jamie and his mates. But the deeply gendered distinction between cooking as a vocation, a technical skill and cooking as a domestic chore, as caring work, holds fast.

Sex in the kitchen is still in the missionary position.

TABLE FOR ONE

'It's mostly singles around here,' my friend Leila explained. She was sitting on a worn blue couch in her two-bedroom apartment as we chatted over chardonnay and rice crackers. I remembered when she had bought the place two years ago. It was a stressful time, made more so by the fact that her long-term partner, Ziad, had opted out of buying the place with her. Leila catalogued the singles who lived around her in this neat redbrick housing complex. 'An older single woman called Alexandra lives opposite me. Next door is Sean, a single man in his forties. On the other side, there's another single guy, and upstairs is another, a weirdo I can hear having loud sex and long baths in the middle of the night.' We giggled about this. Mr Weirdo had been playing his saxophone when I arrived at the flat. I could hear his uneven jazz riffs as I walked up the stairs. Sax, sex and suds, I quipped, quite a combination. On the top floor, Leila told me, there were more singles and one married couple without kids. In the building next door it was also all singles except for one married couple, also without kids. This, it appeared, was modern living.

I hadn't come over just to gossip about the neighbours. I was there to talk about food, specifically about how Leila's eating patterns had changed over the years as she moved from family home to flatting with friends, to living with Ziad, to living alone. Leila comes from a Lebanese family for whom 'food is everything.' 'My mother's sole occupation is to cook. It is her number one priority. Every Sunday is family day and the first thing I do when I enter my mother's house is eat.' In a traditional family of three girls and one boy, the girls were recruited as helping hands in her mother's constantly active kitchen. 'We had to learn how to core the eggplant and the zucchinis, peel mountains of potatoes and roll grapevine leaves like there was no tomorrow.' Leila's brother missed out, of course. 'To this day, he can't even boil an egg.'

The first time Leila moved out of home, she was twenty-one years old but quickly boomeranged back to the family hearth due to poverty and near starvation. She moved out again when she was twenty-four, to share a place with her cousin and a couple. Flatting with these three accomplished cooks, she was nevertheless in survival mode when it came to food. 'I didn't know how to cook. Despite all the instruction from my mum, I'd never made a meal from scratch. I ate lots of pasta and sauce. I ate chips and gravy at uni – two dollars and you were full for the entire day. I also lived on whatever Mum cooked and brought over for me.' It was every flatmate for herself in this living arrangement, with each of them responsible for buying their own food. 'My cousin would take pity on me and feed me sometimes,' Leila recalled. When she moved into a different place with her cousin, Leila got some basic instruction. 'My cousin taught me how to make fried rice and pizza. I would make those twice a week, every week.'

Things changed when she met Ziad and they started living together, the start of a seven-year love affair that was now over. Food and eating became an integral part of their relationship, but at the beginning the eating situation was dire. 'When we first lived together we ate out every night at the Thai take-away. He was a student and I was earning $35,000 a year. It was just terrible.' The irony was that at the time, Leila was working as an editor for a publisher specialising in cookbooks. 'I lied the whole time I worked there. I pretended I could cook. One day my boss asked, "When you grill your salmon, how do you keep it moist?" I panicked and said I soaked it in olive oil. I had no idea what I was talking about.' Both Leila and Ziad recognised that they had to learn to cook or face endless servings of Pad Thai. So they started buying fish and going to the food markets. And Leila started remembering how to make simple food, the basics from her mother's kitchen. She began to absorb the meaning of those recipes she was editing. And Ziad started trying out the recipes himself.

Together Leila and Ziad progressed from corner take-away to cooking for each other at home six times a week. 'Cooking was a big deal for us. It was a huge part of our relationship. We taught each other to cook.' Their evening meal evolved into 'a beautiful ritual.' 'I would cook and he would eat and admire my food. Dinner was everything. It was a time together.' In the last few years of their relationship, Ziad, a PhD student, was the household's regular cook, preparing fabulous dinner parties for their friends. Even when they stopped living together, the shared meals continued. 'He would invite me to his flat and make an elaborate meal for me. It was the same kind of thing we shared before.' Leila's eating life was transformed by their break-up. 'I didn't have any food in my fridge. If you asked me what I ate the previous evening, I couldn't tell you. I just didn't care. I ate whatever I could lay my hands on. I ate rubbish. I would eat biscuits or chips for dinner. It was awful.'

As Leila adapted to single life and worked through the grief of a long relationship ending, she started to eat better. After a few grim months, she decided to start looking after herself, returning to the vegetarian meals she had perfected during her time with Ziad. 'It changed the way I feel about myself. I have lost four kilos. My hair was falling out and now it's growing back.' She began shopping every few days for fresh food and started cooking five nights a week (minus Friday nights out and Sundays at her mum's food fest). When I visited the flat, she showed me her recently renovated kitchen. But as a single woman, returning to the rich food culture of her family home or her time with Ziad remained difficult. 'I don't cook properly. I steam veggies or make a salad or a stir-fry. It's not the cooking I used to do. I'm not stuffing vegetables or baking things. I haven't used my oven in six months.'

For Leila there were a number of barriers to cooking 'properly.' Time was the most obvious. 'Cooking is a bit of a burden. When I was with Ziad, it would take up to two hours for me to cook a meal and clean up afterwards. Then I would have no time for myself. Now that I live alone, salads are the key. Maximum time it will take to make a salad is fifteen minutes.' The ritual of dinner also seemed to have been lost. Now, dinner was a meal eaten on the couch watching TV. 'I tried to eat at the table but I felt a bit lonely after the break-up.' Her greatest challenge was to control the amount of food she ate and to avoid using food as a comfort. And then there was the lack of incentive to cook for one when she arrived home late and tired. Leila gestured at the plate of crackers, fruit and cheese in front of us. 'The last thing I wanted to do today, coming home grumpy and hot, was to cook. Chucking together some fruit and cheese is my dinner. That's all I can manage tonight.'

*

Leila is part of a fast growing group of Australians: people living alone. Between 1996 and 2001, the proportion of Australians living alone increased from 2 per cent to 9 per cent. In the next twenty years, the number of people living alone is anticipated to increase from 1.8 million to between 2.8 and 3.7 million. As a proportion of the total population twenty years from now, people living alone will represent somewhere between 12 per cent and 15 per cent. Currently, more than 25 per cent of Australian households are occupied by one person, making this the largest and fastest-growing household type.[1] Single-person households include young men and women asserting their independence, widowed older women and men, and divorced or never-married singles of both genders and all ages.

With the increasing number of people living alone, there is an inevitable increase in people catering for one. This expansion in solo dining has encouraged the market to develop new products and services aimed at hungry singles. An obvious example is the development of snazzy, kitchen-free apartments for singles who rarely have the time or desire to cook. Food products have also been developed especially for the single eater. Many of these are on display at the largest supermarket in Potts Point, an expensive inner-city suburb of Sydney that boasts a concentration of apartment

blocks peopled with well-heeled singles and childless couples. The supermarket knows its neighbours, and their cooking and eating habits, well. As you walk into the place, you
are faced with towers of red plastic baskets and snakes of
mini trolleys; there is no room for those deep, unwieldy
cages you get at 'normal' supermarkets. The other noticeable
difference is the sound. This supermarket is almost tranquil
in comparison to my local family-oriented supermarket. No
teething toddlers or five-year-olds in Superman costumes,
clutching packets of chips and yelling, 'But I want it,
Mummy!' Here, the magazine and travel-accessory sections
are bigger than the baby-supply section; single men and
women wandering the aisles are distracted only by the special offers on imported jams and rice crackers. It's a place
where you can buy gourmet salads for one, small packets of
steamed veggies, Asian stir-fry or baby potatoes, and corn on
the cob for two. The store stocks something called 'quick
bites' – packets of pre-cut carrot and celery sticks and baby
tomatoes. With dip and cheese, this would provide Leila
with an easy mid-week dinner or nibbles for friends before
dinner out. Of course, the freezer section offers the full
range of Lean Cuisines, and Neil Perry sauces to accompany
the single salmon and chicken portions they sell at the deli.
Visiting this place on a Tuesday or Wednesday night, you see
people dressed in suits or office-casual garb rush in and out
in less than twenty minutes, clutching a few items to tide
them over until their next business dinner or restaurant meal
with friends.

Of course, some foodies and health-care professionals
would cluck their tongues at the idea that this kind of eating
constitutes a healthy diet. In the updated edition of *One*

Continuous Picnic, our most comprehensive history of eating in Australia, Michael Symons associates the rise of the single-person household with the continuing decline in domestic eating. He states: 'The health benefits of dining together should never be underestimated, and epidemiologists have found dining alone to be as hazardous as smoking.'[2] From time to time, stories appear in the media telling us how unhealthy the diet of the single person is when compared with the diet of a typical couple or family of four. There is some research to support these claims. The 2004–05 National Health Survey found that Australians living alone were more likely than either couples or families with children to drink heavily and more likely to eat fewer than four servings of vegetables a day. They were also more likely than couples to be sedentary and to eat one or fewer servings of fruit a day. (Interestingly, couples and couples with children were more likely to be overweight or obese than singles).[3]

There are various possible explanations for these apparent dietary discrepancies between singles and couples or families. Age is a factor (many singles are older). So are finances (the cost of living, including housing and utilities, is often higher for singles). Then there is the notion of 'improved behaviours.' The theory is that when you are in a relationship or part of a family you are less likely to drink heavily or indulge in bad foods, either because you are happier or because of the controlling effect of living with others. The 2005 Ipsos Mackay Report *Home Alone* found some evidence to support this 'improved behaviour' theory. That report found that for singles, living alone was associated with freedom, including the freedom 'to eat what you like, when you like.'[4] That freedom may sometimes involve biscuits in bed, midnight snacks, baked beans on toast and comfort food.[5] As some of the participants in the study commented, living alone can involve some unhealthy habits. 'I probably eat less healthy things,' one person admitted. Another thought that living alone meant he tended to 'eat out more and drink more.'[6] Whether or not couples and families are happier and healthier than singles is difficult to prove. But the view persists, among some food and health professionals and singles themselves, that single living can be harmful to your health.

*

While the statistics highlight the potential health costs associated with single eating, there is also the question of the social cost. Despite the increasing number of singles in our community, eating alone, whether in public or in private, seems somehow awkward, not entirely the proper way to dine. Of course, eating and cooking are, and have always been, highly social and rule-bound activities. Food historian Margaret Visser describes them as culturally determined 'ritual movements.'[7] A simple meal, however casually prepared, quickly eaten and easily forgotten, is still an important everyday ritual. But for some singles, the process hardly seems worth it. For Michael, a thirty-something academic and muso, 'there is so much ritual surrounding cooking and eating, the idea of going through all that just to feed yourself seems strange, especially when there are other things to do – the interesting book to read, the important paper to write.' Connected to this idea of ritual is the notion that eating and cooking are basically communal activities, that food is 'a social thing,' to be shared and enjoyed in the sharing. Even singles who love to cook and are adept at it feel a kind of emptiness when they perform the task just for themselves.[8] The links between sociability and eating are hard to unravel, because, as Visser comments, 'we use eating as a medium for social relationships: satisfaction of the most individual of needs becomes a means of creating community.'[9] The connection between eating and human relationships is embedded in our language. As Visser observes:

> We still remember that breaking bread and sharing it with friends 'means' friendship itself, and also trust, pleasure, and gratitude ... Bread as a particular symbol, and food in general, becomes, in its sharing, the actual bond which unites us.[10]

The flip side of this is that eating alone, despite the fact many more of us are doing so, retains some of its stigma. In public, at a restaurant, many singles report feeling 'strange' or 'odd' eating out by themselves. If forced to eat on our own, we come with reading material at the ready or we fiddle with our mobiles or leaf through our diaries, hoping to avoid what one assumes are the pitying looks of fellow diners. At home, the TV newsreader or sitcom family is the single's dinner companion. Ironically, at the very time when it would be nice to be invited out to dine, those who are newly single report a drop in dinner-party invitations. It's as if we can't set the table for five, without inviting another stray single for matchmaking purposes.

The idea that food is intrinsically communal is at the heart of Adam's food story, a story he shared with me in exchange for a home-cooked Italian meal. We chatted over ravioli and salad in his rented art deco flat near the beach, where he was living on his own. At the time of our dinner, Adam was a thirty-something public servant. He grew up in a large family that loved food; his dad was in charge of the barbecue and his mother was 'the best domestic cook ever.' 'Family meals were always shared together at the table,' he explained. 'They were a ceremony, there was a lot of talking. It was a very strong tradition in my family, a very social time.' Once out in the world, flatting with mates or on his own, living in college or travelling the world solo, Adam's eating habits were of a somewhat lower standard than when he had been living with his parents or in a serious relationship. That's because for Adam, as for many other singles, cooking takes on a different character when done with or for another person:

> If you are cooking for yourself, it's a chore. Cooking for someone else, there's pleasure involved. When you are with someone, it's a dialogue about what you are going to eat. When you are on your own, you come home tired and think, what is there that's quick? It's generally fatty with not much greenery involved. Having someone else to cook for, the social process of cooking means it's much more fun to take the time to do it properly. When you are by yourself it's an indulgence – you indulge whatever good or bad tastes you have.

At the time of our ravioli dinner, Adam was living alone but in the first few months of a serious relationship; they had just started spending most nights together, either eating out or at each other's apartments. As a consequence, Adam was eating better food and cooking more. 'Living with a partner, you definitely eat more regularly and eat healthier food,' he concluded.

*

When you ask single people why they don't cook more often, a common response is 'lack of time.' This indeed was Ian's reason. A local councillor and office manager, Ian considered cooking every evening to be too much effort, especially when he had meetings scheduled at least three evenings a week. 'I try to cook a roast on the weekend and reheat it during the week,' he explained. 'One chook gives you a dinner and a couple of lunches. Or you just go to Woolies for one of their barbecued chooks and some frozen veggies.' But even this can seem like too much effort. 'Sometimes, by the time you get a park, find the stuff and queue up, you are over it.' Adam felt the same way. For him a normal eating day consisted of coffee for breakfast, a take-away sandwich for lunch consumed in front of the computer, and dinner at a restaurant, quick and easy pasta or take-away. 'It's not that I don't enjoy cooking,' he told me. 'I just don't want to cook and clean up. By the time you get home at 7 or 8 p.m., shop for food and then actually cook the meal, you've lost half of your appetite. Then you have to clean up the mess.'

Of course, 'lack of time' is the same reason for not cooking more proffered by working parents, busy university students, executive couples and most of the employed population. But I think there might be something more at work here for singles. Perhaps, instead of cooking, many singles would rather do other things, things that feel more 'natural' to do on your own and for yourself: exercising, watching TV, reading or working. Or is it that many singles believe the kind of cooking they have to do (quick and easy, and for one) isn't 'proper' cooking? Leila lives on home-made salads for dinner but doesn't consider this 'proper' cooking. Adam believes that cooking for two means you take the time to cook 'properly' instead of simply heating up some pasta and sauce. And so we cling to this idea of 'a proper meal' as something that is eaten at a table, home-cooked and shared with others.[11] If something is 'proper' it is 'suitable,' 'correct' or 'genuine.' Another way to define 'proper' is 'excessively respectable.' The cooking singles do is, in their own eyes, neither real nor respectable.

The question of what constitutes 'proper' cooking brings up a somewhat controversial debate within the discipline of home economics about the state of domestic cooking skills in countries like Australia. This debate has intensified in recent years in the face of people's increasing reliance on industrially prepared convenience foods. On one side of this debate are those who are concerned about the fate of cooking skills. They emphasise the idea of cooking from scratch using 'proper' techniques such as braising or casseroling, jointing a chicken, making a white sauce, cooking beans and pulses and making short-crust pastry. Then there are those who take a broader view, who believe cooking skills in countries like Australia are in transition. They argue that cooking has had to change in response to changes in family structure, work commitments and, particularly, the role of women.

One of those people taking the 'skills in transition' approach is British academic Frances Short. In a research paper drawing on interviews with thirty cooks living in England, Short argues for a 'person-centred' approach to cooking skills. Instead of applying a rigid and traditional definition, Short takes a more expansive view, which takes into account the individual doing the cooking. This kind of cooking might combine 'cooking from scratch' with 'cooking with pre-prepared foods.' An example of this would be putting together a salad using canned chickpeas, or making burritos using roast chicken from the supermarket. Instead of fretting about the 'right' way to poach an egg or make dressing, this flexible approach to domestic cooking considers broader questions: Is the food nutritious and healthy? Is it economically accessible? Does it suit the lifestyle of the individual? The answers to these questions, rather than the complexity of the chef's techniques, provide the best insight into contemporary cooking habits.

And what about the other skills developed by the modern domestic cook, skills which rarely make it into the cookbooks and cooking shows? Cooking while doing other things at the same time (helping the kids with their homework; talking to a work colleague; paying bills online). Cooking under stress (preparing a dinner party for six on a weeknight in under forty-five minutes; cooking with small children underfoot). In Short's study, she found one of the most important modern cooking skills involved 'creative efficiency': the ability to prepare an evening meal, for instance, that can be adapted with other ingredients and served, in a slightly different guise, the following day (as Michael does with his weekend roast). This person-centred approach to domestic cooking skills highlights the 'capabilities and practices of the cook' rather than the 'requirements of the cooking-task.' As Short argues:

It seems perverse to argue that the person who occasionally makes scrambled eggs to a consistency deemed 'correct' by food writers and television chefs is more or less skilled than the person who regularly prepares a pasta dish for their family with a chilled, pre-prepared pasta sauce from the supermarket and 'what's left in the fridge.'

If we take Short's approach to cooking skills, then Leila's salad, Michael's recycled roast and Adam's quick pasta are all worthy of being described as 'cooking.' And if we adopt such a 'person-centred' approach to cooking, the deep concerns among home-economics teachers and foodies that cooking skills are in decline seems like an over-exaggeration of sorts.

Singles themselves, however, don't always see things this way; several of the people I interviewed dismissed their meals as not 'proper' cooking. The attitude of singles to their own single status can aptly be described as 'conflicted.' On the one hand, they enjoy the freedom of living alone, the capacity to choose between intimacy and solitude, to pursue their own interests and passions without the need to factor in the requirements of others. But this sense of independence comes with other, darker preoccupations: vulnerability, insecurity and loneliness. For many singles, living alone is something that just happened, rather than a planned event. And then, the more philosophical question: Are we meant to live alone? The psychological angle: What does my single status say about me? Single people's attitudes and habits in relation to cooking and eating reflect these conflicts. In thinking that cooking is not worth doing for one, that throwing together a quick salad or pasta isn't 'proper' cooking, singles are almost saying 'I'm not worthy.' Not bothering to cook for yourself may well be evidence that you are in a kind of holding pattern, as if you were biding your time until another person came along to justify a casserole. But what if the permanent dinner guests aren't due to arrive for a long time, if ever?

*

The TV program *Sex and the City* celebrated the fabulousness of single women, at the same time acknowledging the web of doubts, fears and annoyances associated with living alone. In one episode, sassy lawyer Miranda nearly chokes on a dumpling while watching bad TV. She panics at the thought that she will die alone and that her cooling corpse will be gnawed at by her cat. In another episode, entitled 'They Shoot Single People, Don't They?,' the usually über-confident Samantha is stood-up in a restaurant. She sits amid a sea of dining couples without any of her 'dining alone armour' (a book, a work project or a magazine). Exposed and vulnerable, she accidentally tips over a wine glass and flees the restaurant in tears (but not before pashing the bus boy on her way out). Sam's experience leads Carrie to pose the question: should restaurants be divided into singles and non-singles, like the smoking and non-smoking sections of yore? The episode ends, like all the goods ones did, with an affirmation that it is better to be on your own than to put up with a mediocre relationship. In the final scene of that episode, Carrie, determined to be truly comfortable with her single status, sits by herself with her glass of wine at a sidewalk restaurant table. 'No armour, no man, no faking.'

As these scenes illustrate, many singles, despite their increasing numbers, still feel self-conscious eating alone in public and have to work hard to overcome the stigma of single dining. Even in the privacy of their own homes they require the company of the television. Some of these feelings might boil down to their own conflicted feelings about their single status. Indeed, the attitude of singles to cooking and eating shows us that our food choices are not dictated solely by cost and availability. There are deep social and emotional reasons why we eat the way we do. These reasons even influence the way we view time. How many Australians living alone might make more time to cook if they were catering for others? But singles' ambivalent attitudes to cooking are also a reaction to how they are viewed in our society. Despite decades of social change, the idealised version of what constitutes a family or a household still stands firm. And despite the fact that elaborate cooking is done less and less by more and more Australians, single or otherwise, we still cling to the notion that that's what 'proper' cooking is all about. Until this perception changes, singles like Leila, Ian and Adam will continue to think cooking isn't worth doing when there is just one person at the dinner table.

BUSH TUCKER NO MORE

JJU Charcoal Chicken take-away is conveniently situated next to the old courthouse on Redfern Street, just a few paces away from the Aboriginal Medical Service. It's a run-down joint to say the least. The day I visited, the sky-blue interior and white tiles were smudged with grime from the chickens cooking over the coals, suspended in horizontal pirouettes. I walked straight to the drinks fridge and grabbed a fruit juice; the juice was nestled among Cokes and Fantas of all possible sizes. I found a free plastic chair and table for one and contemplated the blackboard menu. I could get an egg and bacon roll for $3.50 or a roast chicken with chips and gravy for $5.90. A chicken and salad roll would cost me more than that, $6.40. As I considered what to order, a mountain of a man in a beanie and tattered jumper started to sing to me. 'You know what I want, you know what I need ...' I decided to stick with just the juice and forgo the food on offer. At the table next to mine an elderly man in a fedora read the *Telegraph* while drinking a Pepsi and munching on a Chiko Roll. It was 9.30 in the morning; perhaps this was his usual breakfast fare. I had come to JJU Charcoal Chicken because I had been told that it was popular with the locals. I finished my juice quickly, scribbled a few notes and left, feeling a little self-conscious and more than a little greasier than when I had arrived.

In order to visit JJU Charcoal Chicken take-away I had to travel though the heart of Redfern, home to the largest concentration of indigenous people in metropolitan Sydney. Barely five minutes' drive from the up-and-coming inner-city suburbs of Surry Hills and Alexandria, Redfern has been the scene of ugly confrontations between police and the inhabitants of 'The Block,' a housing estate bound by the streets of Eveleigh, Vine, Lois and Caroline. This area is currently being 'revitalised' by a relatively new government organisation, the Redfern-Waterloo Authority, which is promising urban renewal, improved human services and job creation.[1]

For some time now Redfern has been changing at the edges, owing to its proximity to gentrified suburbs like Darlinghurst and the insatiable hunger for property close to the city. In some streets, you will find expensive new apartment blocks and up-market cafés. In one of these cafés, I met up with Jennice Kersh, the former co-owner (with her brother Raymond) of Edna's Table. Edna's was a fine-dining restaurant in the CBD of Sydney that had a unique approach to Australian food. It was one of the few top-notch restaurants in the country to use bush foods in all its dishes. Dishes like kangaroo-tail broth, red-ball chillies stuffed with emu, lamb poached in paperbark with lemon myrtle, and wattle-seed crème brulée. The morning we met, Jennice seemed to be hyper on coffee. Or perhaps that's how she is normally. Dressed in tight jeans, a lacy top and strand upon strand of shell jewellery, she was full of the urge for storytelling. She spoke to me at length, with a mixture of excitement and disappointment, about the rise and demise of Edna's Table and the mixed success of 'bush food' in Australia.

Edna's Table hadn't always been a native-food restaurant. When it first opened in the early 1980s on Kent Street, in the heart of Sydney's business district, all Jennice and Raymond wanted to do was serve adventurous Australian cuisine. They tried to source meat like kangaroo, but at that stage it was illegal to serve it in restaurants.[2] They struggled to get native ingredients commercially. The existence of commercial and legal barriers to the consumption of bush foods comes as no surprise. Bush tucker has never been widely popular with white Australia. Australia's first cookery book, published by a Tasmanian called Edward Abbott in 1864, did included numerous recipes for kangaroo, including stuffed kangaroo, jugged kangaroo and kangaroo pastie.[3] In the early days of transportation, some convicts embraced native foods, especially kangaroo meat, as a useful source of protein.[4] For the most part, however, respectable free-settler society remained either uninterested in or hostile to bush food. As food writer Richard Beckett comments, when non-indigenous people arrived on Australian shores they believed the 'natives' had little to offer in terms of useful food knowledge.[5] Despite the availability of indigenous foodstuffs during 'the hungry years' of the colony, many starving new Australians found this produce 'culturally unacceptable.'[6] Salted pork and rock-hard biscuits, it seems, were more palatable than witchetty grubs and bush tomatoes.

The first Edna's Table closed in 1989. When planning to re-open in the early 1990s, Raymond and Jennice wanted to make native foods an essential part of their menu. They had been inspired to create a quintessentially Australian cuisine by their stay at Balgo Hills Mission Station in the Kimberleys. Of course, the early 1990s seemed like a good time to open a restaurant celebrating indigenous culture. These were eventful times. The Aboriginal and Torres Strait Islander Commission was established in 1990 as an elected body responsible for the federal Aboriginal-affairs budget. The next year the Council for Aboriginal Reconciliation was set up to focus on the broader relationship between indigenous people and other Australians. In the same year the *Mabo* decision was handed down by the High Court, giving *sui generis* rights over crown land to indigenous peoples who could prove a continuous connection. The *Native Title Act* passed in December the following year.[7] Twelve months prior to that, Paul Keating had delivered his famous Redfern Park speech, five minutes down the road from JJU Charcoal Chicken. He talked about justice for past injustice, about forging a new partnership between indigenous and non-indigenous people. 'We cannot confidently say,' he opined, 'that we have succeeded [as a nation] if we have not managed to extend opportunity and care, dignity and hope, to the indigenous people of Australia.'[8] In the early 1990s, there was a feeling that Australians might be willing to atone for the past and open up to what our indigenous cultures had to offer.

Nevertheless, Edna's owners were having trouble converting people to the cause of bush tucker. Jennice and Raymond wanted to rename their restaurant 'Narmaloo,' after a waterhole at Balgo Hills. They were granted special permission by the people of Balgo to use the name. But the managers of the building that was to house the new restaurant were less enthusiastic. To them it sounded 'too ethnic.' As Raymond explains in their cookbook: 'They tried to tell us politely that they wanted the same Edna's Table that had been at

Kent Street or something European, preferably French.'[9] In the end Raymond and Jennice stuck with the name Edna's Table II. Edna's the sequel. Only it wasn't, because everything from the menu to the interior was inspired by Aboriginal culture.

In the literature on bush food at the height of its popularity, aspirations for the cuisine were high. In her chapter on bush tucker, Cherry Ripe quotes Andrew Fielke, the owner of Adelaide's Red Ochre Grill: 'The bush-food industry is really poised to take off,' he proclaimed in 1993. 'It's going to be huge.'[10] The Kershes were even more ecstatic in their cookbook, published in the late 1990s. They believed that bush tucker would soon be part of our everyday diet. 'One day our children will take sandwiches to school filled with warrigal greens, kangaroo prosciutto and wild Davidson plum chutney.' More than that, bush tucker would unite indigenous and non-indigenous people in a kind of commercially inspired reconciliation:

> Raymond and I have a dream that one day adventurous farmers in Western Australia and North Queensland will work together with Aboriginal people to create a great local and export food industry. I can think of no better way to further the process of reconciliation.[11]

As the decade progressed, this interest waned and resistance to bush food remained strong. As Jennice told me when we met: 'We thought if we created this beautiful restaurant, and we had a didgeridoo playing while Joe and Joanne Bloggs celebrated their thirtieth wedding anniversary, then they were accepting indigenous culture.' But it was a thin kind of acceptance. These native ingredients put off the average Australian diner, even the sophisticated ones. Some foodies, critics and industry colleagues were dismissive of bush food. And while friends and supporters continued to come to Edna's, the question was often asked: 'Why are you cooking that bloody blackfellas' food?' 'I used to think, what must it be like to be black in this country? If I feel disheartened and rejected because they won't eat our food, what must it be like for them?' It was hard, in the end, to shift the image of bush food as something squirmy and unappealing that some bearded bloke in khaki shorts pulls out from under a log.

Looking back, Jennice believes the dream she shared with her brother of bringing a greater acceptance of indigenous culture to white Australia through food was naive, even arrogant. She admits that although she has dedicated much time and energy to understanding the indigenous way of life, her experience with that culture has only ever been partial:

> You can cook with native ingredients, you can own an indigenous restaurant, you can be very good friends with [Aboriginal rugby champion] Mark Ella, you can visit the bush, but then you don't actually know any indigenous people in your own neighbourhood. I've lived in Redfern since 1994 and I had never been on the Block until fifteen months ago. Because I'm scared. I was mugged by a few Aboriginal men coming out of the station a few years ago.

At the beginning of the flurry of interest in bush tucker, Cherry Ripe wrote that the traditional foods of indigenous people had 'hardly become mainstream' or 'made great inroads into the national diet.'[12] It is even more so a decade later. The sorry reality is that when it comes to indigenous food today, we are not talking about Kakadu plums or crocodile meat, but hamburgers, chocolate bars and cans of Coke.[13]

*

Leafing through back issues of the *Koori Mail*, the indigenous community's national newspaper, provides a sobering picture of indigenous health. You spot story after story about diabetes, heart disease, hospital admission rates and poor nutrition. Reading through these stories and the endless reports on the health problems of indigenous people, you uncover harsh realities in the form of bare figures and statistics. Sixty-one per cent of indigenous Australians are classified as overweight or obese compared with 48 per cent of non-indigenous people.[14] Hospitalisation rates for type-two diabetes for indigenous males and females are ten times those for other Australian males and females.[15] The incidence of gestational diabetes among indigenous women may be as high as 20 per cent.[16] Not to mention the figures associated with indigenous life expectancy and birth weight.[17]

Whether young or old, living in urban or remote communities, Aboriginal Australians are far more likely than non-Aboriginal Australians to suffer from a range of diseases associated with poor nutrition and obesity such as kidney disease, heart disease and diabetes. The problems worsen as you move away from the cities. Indigenous Australians living in remote areas are more likely to have diabetes than their urban cousins. In the Northern Territory, type-two diabetes affects one fifth of the indigenous population. In his study of the small Territory town of Lajamanu, anthropologist

Erik Saethre found residents diagnosed with type-two as young as fifteen years old.[18] As Nicolas Rothwell asserts in his book *Another Country*, kidney failure is 'a sickness sweeping across remote Aboriginal Australia,' a 'plague, [a] crisis, [and an] epidemic.'[19] He describes this landscape as 'a place where community leaders abruptly sicken, disappear to far-off towns for treatment, and die; a place where funerals are weekly affairs, the clinic is the hub of life, and customs and traditions are passed on under a bleak, mocking shadow.'[20]

It seems that the problems with indigenous Australia are mirrored in developed and developing countries around the world. While obesity and diabetes rates have risen across the globe, they have been particularly bad in what science journalist Ellen Ruppel Shell calls 'traditional cultures in transition' in Polynesia and Micronesia and amongst indigenous and emigrant populations in the United States, Fiji, South Africa, Britain, Singapore, Taiwan and Hong Kong.[21] In these places, the 'brutish assault of rapid Westernisation' has brought about a transition in food consumption and lifestyle, a shift from a hunter-gatherer diet to a diet dominated by processed foods, high in sugar and fat. The consequent rise in diseases such as diabetes and high blood pressure has been called 'New World Syndrome.' More than famine and viruses, New World Syndrome is becoming our biggest global killer.[22] At present, it is causing havoc amongst indigenous populations such as ours in Australia.

*

To understand the root causes of this current health crisis, I first have to look to the past. At least that's what Norma Ingram tells me.

When I met Norma, she was working for the Redfern-Waterloo Authority in the human services division. Formerly executive director of the NSW Aboriginal Land Council, she had been actively involved in Aboriginal affairs for over thirty years, holding leadership positions in health, education, children's services and housing. The day we met, we sat down in one of the cool, quiet meeting rooms in a community centre close to the Authority's offices. Norma was pretty cool and quiet herself. She had that calm facade of someone who has spent her life leading and looking after others. I started the interview by asking her what kind of food issues the indigenous community in Redfern was facing. Norma responded by telling me something of the food history of indigenous Australians. Naturally, her own story is tied up with this history as well.

Before white settlement, indigenous Australians enjoyed an organic and healthy diet.[23] They ate berries, seeds, leaves, bulbs, roots and fruits. They ate low-fat meat like kangaroo as well as fish, emu, goanna, birds and grubs of various types.[24] Theirs was primarily a vegetarian menu, as Norma explains, about 20 per cent meat and 80 per cent vegetables and fruits. What's more, they had to exercise hard to get the food, particularly the game, and so they remained fit as well as nourished. Their bodies were lean, designed to keep going with minimal food when supplies were short.[25]

Everything was transformed by white settlement, as indigenous people 'drifted into the mining settlements, stations and coastal towns' or came under the 'protection' of the Church or the State. They lived on mission stations or government reserves. They became divorced from the 'complicated skills and culture which had sustained them perhaps

40,000 years.'[26] New generations grew up without much knowledge of traditional foods or the skills to catch, collect or prepare them. As children were stolen and families dispersed, food production and consumption were similarly disrupted.[27] As Charlie Walkabout, chairman of the Mutitjulu community close to Uluru, told Nicholas Rothwell: 'Traditionally, men would live on kangaroos and bush foods … We've lost the way of taking care of ourselves with foods from the lands – the way people could maintain their wellbeing by cooking the right things.'[28]

This traditional diet was replaced by a near total dependence on rations and 'white' food.[29] Thus were indigenous Australians abruptly 'brought into the fringe of industrial society,' with devastating consequences for their long-term health and wellbeing. Their diet now consisted of white flour for damper, white sugar for tea, camp pie (tinned corn beef), salt and beer, a combination Symons describes as 'the classical nutritional disaster of industrialisation.'[30] In his book *Convicted Tastes*, Richard Beckett tells a story (which may or may not be apocryphal) about a 1950s anthropological study of an indigenous tribe. The investigating team spent a good deal of their time 'preventing bored tribesmen from sneaking away from the declared hunting ground, going back to the mission store and obtaining sacks of flour and rice.'[31]

Norma's own story illustrates the extent to which indigenous Australians were stripped of their original skills, knowledge and self-sufficiency. Born in Cowra on a government reserve, Norma was the youngest of eleven children: seven girls and four boys. The brothers are gone now, but the sisters are still living. Norma believes Aboriginal people's

current health problems stem from the diet they were forced
to eat on missions and reserves:

> Within those reserves, you couldn't go out and buy
> food. It was very restricted. You couldn't own animals.
> Some had veggie gardens, but most didn't. The food
> you got was very, very poor. It was basically sugar, flour
> and tea, the worst kind of diet you could possibly have.

The government gave Norma's mother a meagre sum of
money to buy food and what food could be bought was
strictly monitored. Norma vividly remembers the simple act
of weekly shopping as an exercise in state control and surveillance:

> My mother wrote out a list of food and I would have to
> take it over to the mission manager where he would go
> through that list to check it. Then I would take it down
> to the store. I would get the food but I would have to
> take it back to the mission manager for him to check
> again. So, for example, if we wanted butter, he would
> veto that, because the government was paying. So you
> were allowed margarine, brown sugar, syrup and pow-
> dered milk. Very rarely do I recall eating fruit and veg-
> etables. For breakfast you would have white bread with
> black sauce or tomato sauce.

For Norma, the poor diet of her childhood was not just
the consequence of government cost-cutting or surveillance.
It was about smoothing the dying pillow. 'We were put on
these reserves because the Australian government thought

we would just die out. But we didn't. They tried their best but we didn't. We are still here.'

By the fifties and sixties, as indigenous people left the reserves and missions and gravitated towards cities, they were forced for social and economic reasons to 'bunk in' with family already settled in urban areas like Redfern. Big families lived in small houses without money or the skills to gain employment. Raised on mission food and government rations, once on their own, they maintained the bad culinary habits of the past, clinging to the foods they were familiar with. It's inevitable that food preferences are shaped by past experiences, particularly those of childhood. For Norma and her family, these preferences were for porridge heaped with sugar or syrup for breakfast and dinners of sausages or chops cooked in dripping and mince stew with 'dough boys' (dumplings made from dripping, flour and water).

Norma's diet is different now. Lately she has been buying lots of fresh food in an attempt to counteract the effects of the woeful diet of her early years. 'I don't want to end up with diabetes,' she tells me. 'You put five Aboriginal people in a room you would find they are all affected by diabetes. Either they have it or someone in their family does.' Of course, Norma is a relatively well paid public servant living in Sydney; eating well is not as hard for her as for others in her community.

To understand the present state of indigenous eating, Norma told me, I had to talk to Ken Wyatt, the New South Wales Director of Aboriginal Health. In preparation for our interview, I went through some more grim health statistics. Indigenous people are less likely than non-indigenous people to report a medium to high intake of fruit, more likely to consume whole milk rather than reduced-fat alternatives and to add salt to food after cooking.[32] In a recent study of the eating behaviours in an indigenous community in Brisbane, academic Wendy Foley paints a picture of a diet determined by cost, convenience and the pester-power of kids. Not unlike the eating patterns of the rest of the community, I think, only exacerbated by economic disadvantage:

> Consumption of take-aways at home is common for many indigenous people in the community. Fast food has become an important part of the diet because convenience is highly valued. It is not unusual for families or individuals in this community to eat take-away meals several times each week. Some parents say their older children are not interested in cooking and eat too much take-away food. Fast food provides treats, snacks, bribes for children, social food, standby meals when family cooks are ill or busy, regular meals and relaxation from strict dietary regimes.[33]

For Ken Wyatt, the problems facing indigenous people are deeper than a reliance on take-away foods.[34] Three things featured prominently in our talk about the dietary patterns of indigenous people, living in both urban and remote communities: the big family, the funeral and the local store.

Put simply, Aboriginal families are larger than non-Aboriginal families.[35] Ken himself is one of fourteen siblings. So there are more mouths to feed with limited resources. As Ken explained, the numbers in the average indigenous household can fluctuate as people come and go for different reasons:

If there is a big card game on, it can continue for days. While adults are focused on that, kids fend for themselves. The older kids look after the younger ones. A plate of Weet-Bix with milk and sugar is your dinner for the night. If the numbers in the house change, it is not always easy to make the usual meal. It's easier to send a kid down the shops to get ten-dollars worth of chips, with damper or bread or, if it's available, some Chinese fried rice. Or tinned food. You can feed en masse pretty cheaply with food like that.

Resources are stretched to the limit. The number of people in a house can double if there is a funeral to attend. How often does that happen, I naively enquired?

In some communities, there is a death a week. In others, there is at least one a month. The impact on food distribution is significant. If there is a funeral or even just a get together, because social-security payments are fortnightly, you can have extended family members pay to travel to a given point and stay until the next round of money comes in order to get back home.

Both Ken and Norma spend a lot of time attending these funerals. Norma is alive to the irony at the wake afterwards. 'There are these big cream cakes. People are tucking into them, when the person who died may well have died of a heart attack.'

If you have to cater for Christmas numbers on a regular basis, the cost of food becomes your primary concern. And, as I have already discussed, healthier food choices can often cost more than unhealthy ones. If lean mince is $12.95 a kilo, you aren't going to buy that for a family of ten. Indeed, Ken told me that on his community visits around New South Wales, he is served cheaper, fattier cuts of meat, cordial rather than fruit juice, whatever is cost-effective and easiest to store for long periods of time.

This situation is exacerbated in remote communities, where various factors (refrigerated road transport, rising fuel costs and the difficulties caused by the wet season) can drive food prices up to prohibitive levels. For example, during the 2004 wet season, residents of Kowanyama on the Cape York Peninsula were paying $4.50 for a loaf of bread, $4 for two litres of milk and up to $4.50 for a lettuce.[36] This situation is repeated throughout remote Aboriginal communities across the land.[37] As Ken observed:

> You can buy a can of Coke or a packet of chips any-where in the nation for roughly the same price. But an apple can vary from fifty cents in Sydney to three dollars or five dollars in a remote community. Not long ago in Walgett you were paying eight dollars for a lettuce. If Coke can subsidise a can of drink in a rural commu-nity, why can't the government do the same with fresh produce?

Eight dollars for a lettuce versus a large chips, damper and sausages? No contest, really.

For these remote communities, the local store exerts the greatest influence on eating habits. Residents depend on the store and any take-away service available as their immediate source of food.[38] The store also becomes the focal point of social activity in a remote community. Various factors, including space, cost and taste, influence what's on the menu at a remote store or take-away. As Ken explained:

> It's not always economically viable for the local store to store a wide range of products, particularly fruit and vegetables. They tend to go for foods with a long shelf life and quick turnover. In places like Walgett, Lightning Ridge and Bourke, you see local stores getting by on selling fast, processed foods rather than fresh foods. Quality is also a problem. By the time those fresh supplies get to remote towns, the quality is compromised. Some stores may not have adequate storage containers for these foods either.

Ken's comments are echoed in Saethre's study of the Lajamanu community. Saethre found the local store there stocked a limited variety of basic foods. However, even within that small spectrum, indigenous customers bought an even narrower range of products, mainly bread, milk, fresh and tinned meat, cordial and soda. The take-away store next door was the major source of hot meals, mainly lunch and snacks, invariably high in fat, like chips, chicken wings and meat pies. Although the Lajamanu store stocked some healthy alternatives, the residents tended to choose the unhealthy offerings. Taste and familiarity perpetuate the disastrous eating cycle started on the missions and reserves long ago. What Saethre found was that Lajamanu residents gravitated towards the food they grew up with, the 'proper' food of rationing days: sugary tea, white bread and fatty meat.[39]

Meanwhile, more and more of the shops in remote towns like Lajamanu are closing. Some government-supported community stores are going broke, sometimes due to poor management, which gives the state the imprimatur to withdraw funding. The community is left to rely instead on privately owned stores. Although access issues are most acute in remote areas, urban populations also face problems in this respect. As Norma explained to me, if you live in Redfern and have a car, you can drive to any number of shopping centres in the area. But many in the community don't have access to a car. So they have to take public transport to and from the shopping centres. That can be hard if you have kids in tow. You can catch a taxi home but that's more expensive, as is home delivery. So you are stuck buying from the corner stores within walking distance, with the usual mark-ups that exist in those places. No wonder JJs is popular.

*

In Alice Walker's evocative novel *Now Is the Time to Open Your Heart*, a Hawaiian elder speaks to a group of indigenous men about how to return to their authentic culture. The elder points the finger at 'white' food as a destroying force:

> Our diet is a disgrace. All the white bread and mayonnaise. The beer. All the pig and pasta salad … It's killing us … It is all about food, as I see it … The food we eat, how good it is for us. … Some of us are holding on to bad food we ate years ago … and the bad feelings that went with eating it … without any idea that this is the easiest slippery slope to an early grave.[40]

Health experts are urging Aboriginal people to reject 'white' food and go back to the old ways, to eat the bush tucker their ancestors thrived on.[41] Indeed, a number of communities are running 'bush food' programs in schools and hospitals, canteens and neighbourhoods. As Ken told me, the skills are 'still there through the oldies.' In outback communities, people still hunt and eat kangaroo, goanna, game birds and so on.[42] It would be nice to think we could solve the diet-related health problems of black Australia by returning to a bush-tucker menu. But there are other things that could be done. Freight charges could be reduced. There could be an improvement in customised food storage facilities in remote communities. Government and industry could combine efforts to support community-based stores serving quality food at better prices.[43] Similarly these partnerships could assist in setting up and maintaining local vegetable gardens, orchards and food co-operatives. Information about nutrition could be improved, tailored for an indigenous audience.[44] There are also a number of small but powerful projects being run to break the sugar-fat-salt cycle of indigenous eating. Norma runs a small cooking class for young mums in her community. She teaches them how to make a few healthy dishes and then gives the students the ingredients to take home to repeat the recipes for their families – shifting eating habits one recipe at a time.

Rothwell calls diabetes a 'disease of socio-economic disadvantage.'[45] Indeed for both Norma and Ken, a key aspect of any strategy to combat the health problems of indigenous Australia is improved employment prospects. 'Income is the issue,' Ken told me. 'After rent, tobacco, alcohol, petrol, what's left from the fortnightly payment goes to buy food.

Sometimes, if someone in the family is sick, you have to make a decision between medicine and food.' Unemployment remains high in all types of indigenous communities. When compared with the general population, a high proportion of indigenous people rely on pensions of various types. And it seems that in remote communities in particular, residents dish out more of their total income on food than their cousins living in the city.[46]

Cultural studies academic Elspeth Probyn argues that 'ideas about eating and food may reveal the greatest gulf between whites and blacks in Australia, and provide some of the historical reasons about why we are so estranged.'[47] It's true that the diet and diet-related health problems of indigenous people tell us much about the relationship between black and white Australia. We resisted their culture and their knowledge about food. Bush tucker has been little more than a passing fad, a side-show attraction. In return, we've given them the worst our food culture has to offer, the salty, sugary, fatty foods of the reserve, the mission and the take-away shop. And it's killing them, as much, if not more than, the grog, the cigarettes and the other social problems consequent to colonisation. What indigenous people have lost is obvious: their health, their traditional way of life, their traditional skills and knowledge and their connection to the land. But what have we lost? By scorning bush tucker and dismissing indigenous food knowledge when we first arrived, we lost our chance to learn more about this arid land and about the produce it sustains so easily, produce that is generally low in fat and salt and rich in vitamins. And so, as Richard Beckett points out, 'a cuisine based on products the land had to offer died before it even had a chance to get started.'[48] As our country continues to be hit hard by drought and water shortages and as food prices rise, we may yet be the ones who live to regret it.

LEBS MAKE THE BEST LAMB

In September 2006 there was a particularly intense episode of the SBS television program *Insight* on the topic of Australian values. What are Australian values? Are they unique to our country? Do our values shift over time? The show's audience included representatives from ethnic community organisations, commentators and journalists, politicians and comedians as well as 'ordinary' citizens. This discussion of Australian values developed, perhaps inevitably, into a debate about multiculturalism and particularly the place of Muslim-Australians in our society. There were the usual themes raised – tolerance and acceptance, community and difference, law and culture, racism and equality. At a late stage in the proceedings, journalist David Marr made the following comment:

> In our hearts we know that the best people for cooking lamb in the world are Lebs. They have the best lamb recipes. It's just a joke to think that my grandmother's leg of lamb beats the kind of recipes you get from the Middle East.

There were hearty chuckles of agreement from the Anglo members of the audience following Marr's praise for the shish kebab, but what of the other participants? The camera cut to a somewhat strained smile on the face of a young Muslim man. Marr would be the last to argue this overtly, but his comment gave the impression that the best contribution migrants have to offer Australia is better recipes for meat. Earlier on in the program, lawyer and author Randa Abdel-Fattah made this point in relation to the notion of tolerance: 'If I was born and bred here, why are you having to put up with me as though I'm an annoying house guest?' More than that, it appears – an annoying house guest who must cook the host dinner.[1]

Marr's comment was typical of a broader, well-worn story about the enriching influence of multiculturalism and migrants on how Australians cook and eat. The story goes something like this: until the 1970s, the Australian food scene was all 'cake and steak' (to quote Patrick White).[2] All Australians had to choose from when it came to dinner was a pitiful spread of chops and mash, mixed grills and pies, stodgy cakes and puddings, over-done roasts and boiled vegetables. As successive waves of migrants hailing from wonderful food cultures (Italians, Greeks, Lebanese, Chinese, Vietnamese and so on) made themselves at home here, and as the federal government's official policy of multiculturalism took hold, a greater variety of food was made available to the wider Australian community. The Anglos lapped up all the pasta, hummus, yum cha, laksa and green chicken curry they could as a welcome relief after decades of shepherd's pie and charred lamb chops. This love of ethnic food was a reflection of Australians' increasing acceptance of ethnic diversity and of migrants themselves. Indeed, the migrants' tasty food softened the Anglo population up for the wider societal changes wrought by multiculturalism. Now, we all look back at the bleak Australian food scene prior to the 1970s and think, 'Thank heavens for Al Grassby.'

This basic narrative about multiculturalism and food has been – and remains – pervasive in writing and commentary about food, culture and politics in Australia. Consider the following comments from the introduction to former Labor premier of South Australia Don Dunstan's cookbook, published in the mid 1970s:

> For the most part, before the Second World War, our cuisine reflected the decline into which the average English cook of the nineteenth century had sunk. After the war, the influence of migrant groups … influenced Australian food habits for the better.[3]

Two decades later, food writer Cherry Ripe told a similar story in her book *Goodbye Culinary Cringe*. Arriving in Australia in the 1960s at age twelve, Ripe found that Australian eating was 'still very much Anglo-Saxon fare: roast beef on Thursdays, fish on Fridays and sausages for breakfast.' This dull menu was, thankfully, transformed by migrants, who created 'potentially the most exciting and eclectic cuisine in the world, one that borrows from everywhere.'[4] These foreigners brought an end to the 'white Australian food' era and ushered in a new age of colourful and spicy eating delights.

But it isn't just foodies and food writers who tell this story about migrants remaking the Australian palate. In a letter to the editor of popular food magazine *Delicious*, Helen Ching from Ngunnawal gives her own family's perspective on the transformation of Australian food from pedestrian to cosmopolitan:

> I've grown up with stories from my Romanian grand-mother of how limited the variety of food was when they arrived in Australia in 1952. In 1965, when my Chinese father opened his restaurant, he did mixed grills and sausages and mash as well as the usual Chinese fare of the times. Obviously, tastes back then were not as adventurous as they are today. Throughout the years I have watched with keen interest the development of food in Australia's multicultural society and am proud that we now have a true 'melting pot' of cuisines which is so widely accepted.[5]

Even for those in the Muslim community who have criticised Australians for their lack of racial tolerance, food and multiculturalism are intertwined, as this *FHM* interview with Sheikh Taj el-Din al-Hilaly shows:

> FHM: Is it ironic that 90 per cent of kebabs that are consumed in Australia are scoffed by drunk Aussie guys outside pubs at closing time?
> Al-Hilaly: That's one of the benefits of multicultural-ism – it gives you a much wider diet! The people of the Middle East have failed industrially but they've been very successful in the kitchen, ha ha![6]

With all this in mind, it seems an easy step from 'our food has been changed by migrants' to 'migrant food has changed us.' A 2006 study of national food habits showed that more

Australians are feasting on dim sims, sushi, rice and noodle dishes than on traditional fast foods such as chips, pies and burgers.[7] Take this fact and combine it with the recent data from opinion polls on Australians' views about migrants, and we find that that the majority of those polled generally feel migrants have made Australia a better place. It should be noted, however, that in many of the polls on this topic, fewer people support migrants (and particularly an increase in immigration levels) than consume ethnic food. For example, a May 2006 Ipsos poll found that only 54 per cent of respondents felt migrants were having a positive influence on the country, far less than the 75 per cent who had a preference for dim sims over chips.[8]

It's hard to disagree with the argument that Australia's food culture has been improved by the influence of food traditions from overseas. It's wonderful to enjoy, as *some* neighbourhoods do, a wide choice of restaurants and take-aways serving everything from Moroccan and Japanese to Southern Italian and Mexican. It's great to be able to buy curry paste, rice paper, feta cheese and refried beans in most local supermarkets. But this upbeat story about our cosmopolitan food culture can tend to gloss over some important historical facts, such as the racism suffered by Chinese and Greek Australians who ran cafés in Australian suburbs and towns. These new Australians often cooked Anglicised versions of their native dishes for their customers or avoided serving anything resembling their native cuisine at all.[9] White Australians might have developed a taste for Chinese cuisine, but they continued to consume their sweet and sour pork in a social and political atmosphere in which xenophobia and racist government policies persisted.[10] In many country towns from the mid 1930s until the late 1960s, the local Greek café provided Aussies with 'a sense of community' and 'a social centre as well as an eatery with extended hours.' And yet those Greek men and women who provided this welcoming space were not shielded from racist attitudes or from being called 'greasy spoon dagos.'[11] It remains the case today that we should not suppose too close or too simple a link between the availability of ethnic food and the acceptance of ethnic diversity. Food academic Jean Duruz makes the point that while King Street in Sydney's Newtown, a very popular restaurant strip, may offer a range of culinary styles (African, Balkan, Creole, Malaysian, Portuguese and Sri Lankan), ABS statistics show that the vast majority of the 12,000-odd residents in the area speak only English. As Duruz writes, 'There are no Thai residents specifically recorded for Newtown, although King Street alone has several Thai restaurants.'[12]

Anthropologist Ghassan Hage has been vociferous in his critique of the way we understand the interaction between migrants and non-migrants via food and eating.[13] Was Australian food before the 1970s really as unvaried and unpalatable as some would have us believe? More importantly – and, for Hage, more problematically – this account of Australian food culture is premised on a power imbalance between the host and the migrant. It is a story that is almost entirely focused on the eater and the diverse and interesting food she now enjoys thanks to multiculturalism. The ethnic cook (not to mention the ethnic food grower or kitchen hand) 'is rarely the active central subject' of this story.[14] Hage is critical of what he calls 'culinary cosmo-multiculturalism,'[15] an approach to ethnic diversity based solely on the perspective of the urbane, well-travelled citizen with an appetite for world food and culture. Such a view of multiculturalism has more to do with the availability of ethnic restaurants to consumers with a penchant for international travel than it has to do with the experience of the migrants themselves.[16] It implies that ethnic food and those who cook it have 'no other *raison d'être* than to enrich the Anglo subject.'[17]

Hage's position here is more extreme than my own. Australians' taste for ethnic food should not be dismissed as mere tokenism or snobbery. Rather, it is what Bob Hodge and John Carroll call 'a *social* instance of multiculture.'[18] Put another way, although eating the food of 'Others' in restaurants may be a shallow example of multiculturalism, it is preferable to maintaining a complete and total distance from those Others.[19] What's often missing, however, in the usual story about how ethnic food has enriched the formerly banal Aussie palate is any genuine exchange, any interaction in which, as Hage puts it, 'both the eater and the feeder experience themselves as subjects.'[20] I wanted to see if cultural exchange through food could go beyond 'cosmo-multiculturalism' or 'gastro-tourism' to the exchange of food and experience, knowledge and ideas, caring and friendship.[21] This search led me to a community centre in the Melbourne suburb of Preston, far from the inner-city haunts of the gastro-tourist and urbane foodie.

*

The Spectrum Migrant Resource Centre is located on a main road in Preston. I visited the centre in November 2007 in order to attend one of its lunches for migrant and refugee women. These lunches were being held as part of a project called 'United by Our Experiences,' run by the centre and the Islamic Women's Welfare Council of Victoria (IWWCV). The project's aim was to bring postwar migrant and newly arrived refugee women together over lunch 'to share their common stories and foster greater cross-cultural harmony.' Both the centre and the IWWCV felt postwar migrant communities (Greek, Italian, Turkish, former-Yugoslavian) and newly arrived migrant and refugee communities (Iraqi, Lebanese, West and Central African) needed to get to know each other better. The two organisations had conducted research that showed there was apprehension and concern within these older migrant communities about new migrants, particularly Muslims. The project was born out of a desire to combat these negative feelings. A women's lunch seemed like a good way to approach this. As Stephanie Largos, chief executive of the migrant resource centre, put it to a local newspaper, women are 'the great messengers in the community,' as well as being the ones chiefly responsible for food. Each lunch would feature cuisine from the country of origin of some of the guests. The project's co-ordinator, Siobhan, a young Australian-born social worker, explained to me that although the food wasn't the focus of the project, it did function as a tool to engage the women involved and get them to relax. 'Other organisations have conducted cooking classes and recipe exchanges. But the lunch is all about appreciating other cultures through food, music and dialogue. And food is a comfort thing, especially between strangers. It's the ultimate icebreaker.'

The lunch I attended was to feature food from West Africa, the region of Sierra Leone and Liberia. I was told there were no West African restaurants in Melbourne, although one was starting up soon. So the venue for the lunch was a rather beige meeting room off the centre's reception area, albeit one with photos on the walls of women of different ethnic backgrounds preparing noodles and cooking in woks. Scattered on the plastic table surrounding the water glasses and plates of Assorted Cream biscuits were colourful handouts for use during the day's discussion. When I arrived, Siobhan was busily sorting them, along with name tags and centre information leaflets. The first page of the handout featured the flags of the various home countries of the women attending: Sierra Leone, Iraq, Liberia, Turkey, Macedonia, Greece and the Sudan as well as Australia. The second page listed a number of questions for the guests. Why did you come to Australia? Did you have a choice? What was the journey like? What is it like to raise children in a new country?

I had worried that I would be late, but it seemed I was the first to arrive. Some guests were arriving via public transport; others were being picked up by a courtesy bus. For a while, Lena, an older Greek woman, and I sat in the room flicking through the stimulus material while Siobhan moved in and out like an expectant dinner-party host. Then Fatu and her young companion Fatumata arrived with Fatumata's two young sons. Both women were resplendent in swathes of canary yellow and green, their long dresses covered in tribal motifs and rustic butterflies. The kids were bundled off to another room to be supervised by two Muslim childcare workers. There was colour in the room now, but still mostly silence. Soon the rest of the guests started arriving – two Iraqi women, three older women from Macedonia and a woman in her forties from Greece. The two

Iraqi women sat next to me. The youngest had brought her daughter, leaving her in the hands of the childcare workers in the next room. The two women chatted away to each other, and I heard the word 'childcare' a number of times amid the staccato sounds of their native language. Is there no Iraqi equivalent? Maybe not for what was being offered that day. Throughout the two-hour lunch, I was impressed that the children played without incident, placated perhaps by fruit juice and pizza.

As we enjoyed our appetisers of tea and biscuits, Siobhan started up the conversation. We went around the table introducing ourselves. Fatu and Fatumata were from Liberia. Both had been here for only two years. They didn't need an interpreter because English was their national language, although both also spoke a number of tribal languages. Fatu's English was particularly hard to understand: it took the whole lunch for my ear to get used to her words. As we went around the circle, Siobhan was working hard to get the conversation beyond a somewhat stilted exchange of questions and brief and tentative answers. She wanted the older migrant women to explain to the newly arrived how best to adapt to Australian life. For Lena from Greece, the question was hard to comprehend. 'Work. We come here, we work, get married, have children. That's our life here. It's good.' No one around the table seemed to want to say more than 'It's good here, we are happy,' the obligatory gratitude of those who have been taken in. The conversation soon broke down and the women retreated into private exchanges in their own languages.

Then Janet walked in, a bright spark in jeans and a pink twin-set with sparkles. Originally from Sierra Leone, she had been living in Melbourne for three years. The Liberian women lit up when she arrived and greeted her with excitement and hugs. These women were practically neighbours, as Liberia borders on Sierra Leone; both have had their share of conflict and violence in recent times. Janet had been in Australia three years and had just become a citizen. 'I passed the test!' she announced, her words met with claps from around the table. She had lost her husband in one of the civil wars in Sierra Leone. 'I am here and happy,' she told us.

It was only when Alex, a Lebanese woman in her forties and one of the Spectrum case workers, told her story that I heard something other than 'I'm here and I'm happy.' In her early teens, Alex had to leave all her extended family, her friends, school, her loved and familiar life in Lebanon to come to Australia. She felt nothing but sadness, a deep sense of loss and disjuncture, for years. Now Australia was home, but she had lived an in-between life for much of her teens and twenties. Despite that, Alex still told her fellow lunch companions how fortunate they were. 'When we came here there wasn't much help for migrants. Now there is more support for refugee women. You've come to a country that's welcoming. You're lucky.'

Alex acted as an interpreter for a young woman sitting next to her from the Sudan. She had crept into the room just after Janet's breezy entrance. Shy, veiled and carting along two young sons, she had come a few years ago from the Sudan with three other children. What was life like for her in Australia? She knew she was lucky, but she was also isolated. There was more pressure on her here than back home. Here there was no support, no family, no neighbours. 'If I needed to clean the house, I could get my neighbour to look after the children. If I couldn't take the children to school, they could walk themselves.' This story seemed to give Fatumata licence to admit some of her own unhappiness. 'If you have got family members you could be all right, but being on your own, it's hard.' Fatu felt the isolation too. 'In my country the older women were taken care of and the older women took care of the children. Here no one visits me. Only Janet comes and says hello.' Janet was just as critical of what she saw as the insular nature of the Australian community. 'Back home there would be people to come to see you all the time, making joy, making party. Here no one talks to each other much. When I first came here I noticed neighbours don't talk to each other. I wish someone would talk to me.' Siobhan reassured her that this was also the case for those who were born and bred here. 'I don't know the names of my neighbours, either,' she admitted.

Siobhan then shifted the conversation towards the Iraqi women. How is it different to be a woman here than it is in your home country? Alex interpreted for the women, who were keen to share their thoughts. 'The difference between being a woman here and being a woman is Iraq is like the difference between the earth and the sky,' said the young Iraqi mum sitting next to me:

> In Iraq the man decides everything. There are women who are educated and who work, but still the man decides. The women are not outspoken, they must listen. The man has the power in the family, in the law and in the society. Whereas here there is more freedom. We can divorce our husbands!

Her companion agreed:

Life was okay. We were happy with what we had in Iraq
but there was no security. We were always worried that
our husbands, sons and fathers would be called to war.
Parents always fear for losing a son, wives for losing a
husband.

The group was finally warmed up and it was time for
lunch. Siobhan described the menu of typical West African
food: silverbeet with ground beef, a chicken and mustard
curry, couscous, tomato-flavoured rice, a cabbage salad with
cucumber and sultanas and a black-eyed bean stew with eggplant. I was the first to tuck in. Janet explained that the
eggplant should be eaten with the rice. All the women fol-
lowed suit, piling huge serves on their plates without much
restraint. We talked a bit about where to get the kinds of
ingredients they normally used back home. One woman told
us you could now get the oils and spices they liked to cook
with at the Ghanaian hairdresser up the road.

The caterer of the day's feast helped herself to a plate and
sat down next to me. She was veiled and looked African
but was actually half indigenous Australian, half Fijian. 'I
come from a rainbow family. My son calls himself a fruit
salad,' she said with a chuckle. When she is not catering for
events like this she is conducting nutrition classes for newly
arrived Sudanese refugees. 'They aren't used to the spectrum of fruit and vegetables and other foods we can get
here. They don't know how to cook all this food.' Siobhan
concurred. 'They are generally bewildered by the packaging
and unsure of what to prepare.' Having come from a place

where food was scarce, abundance could create its own problems.

The lunch was drawing to a close and the awkwardness of the first hour had evaporated. Having polished off a few serves of lunch, the Greek and Macedonian women pored over the wedding photos of one of the Iraqi women. She had brought the treasured photos as part of a show and tell, along with the elaborate ceremonial scarves used for dancing at special events. The older Iraqi woman pointed to her son in one of the photos; he was now almost thirty years old, she said. I was surprised. She looked mature, but nowhere near old enough to be a grandmother. 'I was married at fourteen,' she told me, without embarrassment but without joy either. Her own daughter, she said, was married at twenty-three. 'She is studying and waiting to start a family. Too soon for that now.' I thought about the contrast between the lives of her and her daughter. From the earth to the sky.

By now it was time for me to jump in a cab, but before I left I grabbed one of the hand-written recipes that were circulating. It was for the chicken dish with mustard. Janet asked me what Dijon mustard was and where to get it. 'It's yellow and French and you can get it at the supermarket,' was the best advice I could offer her. I went to say goodbye to the Sudanese mum as she wrestled her youngest into a stroller. It turned out she was exactly my age. This woman had five children, ranging from two to fourteen years old. When I told her I was five months pregnant, she reached out to touch my stomach. 'It's so small,' she laughed.

After the lunch, I spoke to Siobhan over the telephone about how the project was progressing. The lunch I had attended was the third in a series of nine lunches with different groups of women from different communities. So far, showcasing various ethnic cuisines had worked well. 'There has been definite curiosity about the food and little resistance to trying the unfamiliar dishes. I thought the older migrant women might react to the spices in the African food but that hasn't happened. What's amazed me is that the women have often remarked "This is like what we eat."' And for the newly arrived migrants, eating food from their country was an important recognition of their own way of life. 'When new migrants come here, they notice that there aren't any restaurants serving their food and they find it hard to get familiar ingredients. But eating their food together with other women, it's an affirmation of their culture.'

I asked Siobhan how the African women she works with had responded to recent comments by the then minister for immigration about their inability to integrate, their low levels of education and, for some, their violent tendencies.[22]

They were pretty upset. A lot of women were calling and trying to work out what it meant for them. Their hopes of family reunions had been snatched from them. I spent a lot of time trying to convince them that valid cases would still be considered. But some women I worked with said they couldn't eat or sleep with the worry.

She also told me that migrants from places like Liberia and Sierra Leone were unhappy about being associated with some violent incidents that had occurred within the Sudanese community. They considered it unfair. They didn't necessarily identify with their fellow Africans or appreciate being lumped into one homogenous group. Indeed, thinking back over the lunch, there was no more affinity between Janet and the young Sudanese mum who rubbed my tummy than there was between Janet and the women from Macedonia. And on the charge of 'inability to integrate,' the strong message I had taken away from the lunch was that these women were desperate to be part of their new community, one that included not just their compatriots but also their new neighbours. It wasn't the free eggplant stew that had brought them to the centre that day, but the chance to get to know others.

As an example of food as a pathway to ethnic tolerance and understanding, the lunch I attended was messy, complicated, disjointed and at times frustrating. It was hard work, much harder than ordering Vietnamese take-away from around the corner. It was a tiring experience, but a much more satisfying one. It had sparked a small but significant conversation between the different women around the table. Food was a conduit, a means of establishing real and potentially transformative relationships between women who had the capacity to share more than just recipes.

*

When my mother's parents first came to Australia from Italy, there was nothing stylish or cool about being Italian. One of the petty incidents of discrimination my *nonna* faced as a young woman growing up in northern Queensland was having to stand at the back of the butcher's shop and wait until all the true-blue customers had been served. One time, sick of being sold yet another substandard cut of beef, she returned to the butcher, package in hand, and firmly asked him, 'Was my money good?' 'Sure,' replied the bemused butcher. 'Well, then why didn't you give me good meat?'

This was a long time ago, of course, and yet my mother, born and bred here and having shed her Italian name through marriage, still feels some of that stigma. I tried to explain to her once that all things Italian were now cool. We were acceptable. We now live in a suburb awash with lattes and Pellegrino, where clothes proudly display their Italian origins and Italian food is popular with gourmands and the hoi polloi alike. It means little to her. 'Sure, they like our food now. Why wouldn't they? It's a lot better than what they were eating before we came. But it doesn't mean they accept us.'

In his book about the history of Italian food, *Delizia!*, John Dickie writes that because so many Italians prior to the 1950s were underfed, the only way they could start eating like Italians was to leave Italy altogether.[23] And so from the 1880s onwards thousands of Italians from north and south left for places like America and Australia. Like the women I met at the lunch, they brought their food traditions to a country where they could finally afford to eat well and where their children could flourish. But if my mother still feels like an outsider after all these years, I wonder how Janet and Fatumata will fare, their children, and beyond, when there isn't even one West African restaurant in their neighbourhood.

WHERE HAS ALL THE
LETTUCE GONE?

Rose Gray and Ruth Rogers are celebrity chefs. They are renowned in the United Kingdom as the owners of the famous River Café restaurant in London and the authors of numerous bestselling cookbooks. The first series of their TV show introduced the world to none other than Jamie Oliver, who was working as a junior chef in the River Café kitchen at the time. Watching their show, I always marvelled at what Gray and Rogers could do with salted cod and chestnut purée (not, I might add, in the same dish). However, when they were challenged by writer Laura Barton to create two of their recipes (smoked eel with samphire and spaghetti with tomato and rocket) using only what could be found in her local supermarket, the chefs were flummoxed. Used to shopping in gourmet stores and organic farmers' markets, they were stumped as they wandered the fluro-lit aisles. Where *do* you find fresh eel in a suburban Sainsbury's? There didn't seem to be any knowledgeable fishmonger waiting to advise them, or any well-stocked fish counter serving plump, yellowish eel with skin intact. Instead they had to rummage through the frozen pork pies and onion bhajis for shrink-wrapped smoked mackerel fillets as a substitute. The search for fresh samphire (sea asparagus, for those who don't know) and horseradish produced similar results, with poor quality substitutes found and fretted over. However, crème fraîche, roma tomatoes and capers were available and the pasta shelves even sported orecchiette. When Laura and the chefs returned home to whip up the dishes, the smoked eel with samphire had been downgraded to smoked mackerel with spinach. The pasta dish was fine, although diminished somewhat by the quality of the olives and oil used. In the end the chefs concluded that if you can't get smoked eel, you shouldn't bother with their recipe.[1]

We know that place affects our access to food and our food choices in complex ways. For instance, consumers notice the different prices between a supermarket in one shopping centre and another store just across the road or in the next suburb. These price differences have also been highlighted by consumer advocates. In 2007, the consumer watchdog CHOICE released a report on food prices based on an analysis of thirty-three staple items in 111 supermarkets across twenty-three Australian cities. They found the cheapest food at a Coles supermarket in the up-market suburb of Prahran in Melbourne. The dearest supermarket was in Dubbo West, where you had to spend an extra twenty-seven dollars for the same thirty-three items. Indeed, CHOICE found the most expensive places for food in New South Wales were in regional areas such as Wagga Wagga, Corrimal and Dubbo.[2]

The question of how the cost, quality and variety of food are influenced by place has been well explored by researchers and writers interested in supermarkets, farmers' markets, local shopping strips, restaurants, cafés, fast-food outlets and roadside diners, any of the sites associated with food and eating. On a more global scale, writers such as Raj Patel have discussed how the world food system shapes the eating habits of local communities as well as entire nations. Concerns about food and place have fueled a social movement advocating local food over food produced by agribusinesses and sold through supermarket chains. The local food movement has helped raise environmental concerns about the 'food miles' racked up when produce has to be shipped long distances from field to fork.[3] Not to mention the impact on quality and on local farming communities.

As intriguing as these issues are, my interest here lies with a smaller, but no less important, question related to how place can influence our access to food in Australia. How is urban development affecting our food supply? The circumferences of our major cities and towns are expanding. The problems with housing affordability don't seem to have seriously curtailed the hunger for generous dwellings with media rooms, backyards and carports. The drought and water crisis are rendering more and more land difficult to farm. Where, amid all of these changes, are the comprehensive plans for domestic food production, particularly in areas close to large population centres? The fate of peri-urban farmers in Australia provides a graphic example of how urban sprawl can affect the dinner plates and shopping trolleys of all Australians. In particular, the demise of market gardens in the Sydney Basin shows us exactly how little some politicians and planners think about our food supply – and about those who supply our food.

*

In the opening paragraph of her book about the history of growing food in Australian cities, academic Andrea Gaynor observes that 'when driving through the streets of almost any Australian suburb today, it is hard to imagine that they were once home to an assortment of agricultural enterprises – a dairy here, a market garden there, a piggery down by the river.'[4] But in the colonial and post-Federation periods, Chinese market gardens stretched from Cairns to the Northern Territory, across Victoria and southern and western New South Wales.[5] In the postwar period, Greek, Italian and Maltese gardeners took over when Chinese populations declined, growing vegetables along the Swan River in Perth and Fremantle and across Victoria and New South Wales. In the seventies and eighties, migrants from Vietnam and Cambodia, many of them refugees, started market gardens in the states where they settled. Before the advent of large-scale farming and agribusiness, thousands upon thousands of market gardens existed in Australia, often close to cities and towns where produce could easily and quickly be transported to hungry customers. The number of farms has slowly been whittled away in recent decades, and in regions like the Sydney Basin, we may see them disappear. Why should this concern us? For one reason, market gardeners in that area currently produce up to 90 per cent of the perishable vegetables consumed by the city's residents.[6]

Travelling through established Sydney suburbs like Epping and Liverpool, passing houses new and old, shopping malls and new developments, it is indeed hard to believe that orchards and livestock existed where there are now cul-de-sacs and perfectly level driveways. Speeding through Kellyville on a cool October morning, I tried to detect the ghosts of trees and cows, but failed. My tour guide for the day, researcher Frances Parker, grew up in the area and recalls its semi-rural past. 'When I was a child Kellyville was full of market gardens. I went to Kellyville Public School and most of my classmates were the kids of migrant market gardeners in the area – Italians, Maltese and Greeks.' Since her family sold up and moved out, the area has changed dramatically. The market gardens are all but gone, replaced by large houses (derisively called McMansions), business estates (including the headquarters of Woolworths) and the occasional Pentecostal church.

Frances is a determined woman. She might look like someone's nana, but she has a fierce and passionate streak that is evident when she starts talking about her life's passion – working with market gardeners in the Sydney Basin. Her journey from Kellyville schoolgirl to advocate for migrant growers was a long one. Frances was one of the first women in the state to do a traineeship in agriculture, after which she went on to be the only woman lecturer at Hawkesbury Agricultural College. Her first engagement with issues facing market gardeners was in the early 1980s, when she became involved in research and community activism on pesticide use by migrant agricultural workers. 'People who only have a weak grasp of English can't read the information on pesticide containers,' she explained to me. 'At the time, 90 per cent of growers in the state couldn't speak English and all of the information was only available in English.'[7] Throughout the 1980s and into the 1990s Frances and some of her students worked with growers from non-English speaking backgrounds – Chinese, Lebanese, Cambodian and Vietnamese – on issues relating to pesticide use. Her work sat uneasily with her peers at the college. They were only interested in broad-acre agriculture like sheep and wheat, not the peri-

urban activities of veggie growers fresh off the boat. Frances
believes that the NSW Department of Agriculture shared
her colleagues' lack of interest in market gardeners; when she
first met with the growers, their only interaction with the
state involved either the immigration or tax departments. It
was through the pesticide project that Frances got interested
in the impact of urbanisation on market gardens. She always
had the sense that the rapidly spreading urban boundaries of
Sydney would pose the greatest threat to market gardens.
'They are under siege,' she told me.

I saw this state of siege myself on the day Frances drove
me to meet some of the market gardeners she has worked
with over the years. Our first stop was Hazlitt Road in Kellyville. Hazlitt Road is frontier country. You can see quite
clearly that this is the edge of a rapidly growing city. There
are horses and goats, market gardens owned and operated by
Chinese and Maltese growers, old fibro shacks and redbrick
houses from the 1960s. These are the remnants of a time
when this road, this area, was all market gardens, a hive of
agricultural activity. Now, enormous, brand-spanking new
houses with satellite dishes are being built all around. Five
minutes back towards the city, you would think you were in
uncompromised suburbia, miles away from livestock and
agriculture.

Halfway down Hazlitt Road, we stopped off to visit a
Maltese lettuce-grower named Frank. Frank's farm (on
which he lives in a weatherboard house with his wife and
adult children) grows all kinds of lettuce using hydroponics.
Most of his farm is covered in netting and on rows and rows
of white tables sit fields of red oak, coral, cos and butter let-
tuces, pristine and perfect, waving slightly in the breeze.

Frances commented that the gorgeous specimens in front of us were far superior to anything she had seen in any of the supermarket chains. Frank agreed. 'You go ten minutes down the road to Kellyville supermarket – the quality is shocking.' (Indeed, we did visit the supermarket there and the red oak was limp and the cos brown at the edges).

Frank chain-smoked through our tour of his farm as he talked about the life of a market gardener. 'As soon as they come, I sell,' he told us. By 'they' he meant the developers, but he might as well have meant the future residents of this area, who will not be gardeners but suburbanites. The area is slowly being overtaken by residential houses and is due to be rezoned residential in the middle of 2008. Farming is a hard life, but one Frank loves and which will continue on through his eldest son, who five years ago bought land in North Richmond in the Hawkesbury area. He will start an organic lettuce farm there. If Frank or his son wanted to relocate to that area now, the land would cost too much. 'That boy, he has his head screwed on, he thought ahead.' But the farming life is drawing to a close for Frank, and he is waiting for a buy-out. He was adamant that he wouldn't settle for anything less than it would cost for him to buy a house close by and retire comfortably. 'This is my super,' he said, gesturing with his calloused hands towards the seedlings and the clumps of green and red leaves. He knows he won't qualify for a pension. The farm is his profession, his home, his past toil and his future livelihood, tied up in six acres. And until the price is right he is not shifting. 'I don't care if they make a building there and there. I am staying. I was here first.'

While Frank was defiant, his neighbour Aldo, a cut-flower grower and third-generation farmer, was resigned, even despondent. Aldo settled in Kellyville in the late 1970s. His grandfather farmed in North Ryde and his father in Peats Ridge. However, the line will stop at Aldo, as his kids aren't keen to adopt the farming life (his daughter is studying law, his eldest son architecture). His youngest son was thinking about taking over the farm, but Aldo discouraged him. 'How can you encourage him when there is no future? There is no good news about farming in the basin. It's dying.' According to Aldo, numerous forces are strangling farming in places like Kellyville. Compared to his father's time, the costs of farming are up and profits down. He used to make $4.50 from a bunch of chrysanthemums in the 1980s, slightly more than he makes now in 2007. Labour supply and costs, especially the price of transport and water, are also daily challenges. But in Aldo's view, the biggest threat to growers is urbanisation. 'Frank Sartor [the state minister for planning] has basically sent us the message you have to be out of here by July next year [when the area is slated for rezoning]. You can't farm in suburbia.' According to Frances, there is tension between growers and nearby residents over fertilisers, spray drift, bad smells, heavy vehicle traffic and the general mess associated with farming. Relocating further away from Sydney isn't viable, not at Aldo's age:

> By the time you finish doing the sums, selling this land, buying new land and setting up there, it's not worth it. And you have to find the right climate. Some places where there is land there isn't water. It's too cold. You spend a fortune on heating and artificial lights. The growers that relocated to the River Flat in Windsor learned that lesson the hard way. It's too cold so they

can only grown in summer because it costs you a fortune to heat in winter.

Aldo's brothers grow gerberas down the road and are in the same boat: 'They can't wait to get out.' And once they all do, it will be the end of many things. 'I am saddened by the fact I am the last generation,' Aldo told me. 'It hurts to know this is it.'[8]

From Hazlitt Road, Frances and I cut across from the north-west towards the south-west, headed towards Austral to visit Christina, a Vietnamese grower. The scenery as we drive along can be described as schizophrenic. One moment you pass a gigantic, newly built shopping centre and housing developments with gates and walls. You turn a corner and you see gardens and paddocks with sheep, handmade signs spruiking organic artichokes and strawberries by the roadside. The area around Austral in south-western Sydney is one of the most important areas for Asian vegetable production in Australia. It has also been nominated as one of the designated growth areas in Sydney under the New South Wales government's Metro Strategy.[9]

Before we went to meet Christina at her home in Bonnyrigg Heights, we stopped to visit her market garden in Austral. The area feels rural, although there are a few residential properties around, 'start-up castles,' as town planner Ian Sinclair calls them.[10] We saw Lebanese cucumbers growing under mesh, Maltese gardens growing potatoes and spinach, and many Asian market gardens cultivating cherry tomatoes and snow peas. You can spot the Asian gardens easily by the women in conical straw hats tending the crops and spraying. Christina and her Cambodian husband grow Asian melons (long, hairy and bitter varieties) as well as Asian herbs, selling direct to restaurants and markets as well as supplying her parents' fruit shop in Cabramatta. Entering her property, we passed two derelict structures, both half-formed Saigon-style two-storey houses. They were intended to be dream homes for Christina and her parents, but the builder went broke before he could complete them. 'Christina is suing the insurance company for the money but it's taking a long time,' Frances told me. The garden itself looked a bit bare; it wasn't yet summer, the peak season for her produce. A few bushes of Thai basil and Vietnamese mint could be spotted but there were no workers around, save one older man who couldn't speak any English and who watched with trepidation as we tried to navigate our car through the mud back towards the main road.

Christina was waiting for us in her driveway in Bonnyrigg Heights. As it was off-season for her, she was only working two days a week, picking and packing her produce. The day we met she was babysitting six young children, her own daughter and son as well as nieces and nephews. Christina is slight, about thirty years old, a mouth full of braces, articulate and vivacious. She sat us down and fed us tea, biscuits and slices of sweet orange. Her family had started farming as soon as they arrived in the early 1980s from Vietnam via a Thai refugee camp. Her parents first grew Asian produce in their backyard, then moved to a larger concern in Horsley Park. But once development started in that area, they felt compelled to move. 'The residents didn't like us. They complained about us spraying crops. It just didn't look like a good future there.' And so they transferred to Austral and then Christina and her partner took over the business from her parents. In summer Christina and her husband start work at six and can remain on the land until eleven at night. They have a few hours break in the middle of the day if it is too hot, time usually spent bunching and packing herbs. Winter days still start at eight so everything can get to the local market in time. They work the property themselves, sometimes hiring a couple of part-time hands in the busy months. It's a hard life, physical and relentless, but like Frank and Aldo, Christina loves it. 'Who would farm if they didn't enjoy it? You don't come from a poor country to come here and do this work if you don't like it.'

The pressures on Christina's business are the same as those on Aldo and Frank's. 'When my parents started, there wasn't a lot of Asian growers around. The produce was easy to sell, not a lot of costs. Now it's hard with the prices of everything, especially water, the laws, the competition. When my parents started years ago you sold a bunch of herbs for four dollars. Now I am still selling that bunch of herbs for four dollars. And my parents didn't have the costs we have.' What worries her most, however, is urbanisation and the fact that her farm is in a targeted growth area. 'You see them with the M7 motorway, all the other development. It's becoming residential. Once they start, it goes like that,' said Christina, clicking her slim fingers. History may repeat itself, like when her family was forced to move from Horsley Park. However, this time it's not clear they will have another place to go where they could sustain crops like melons and herbs. But unlike Aldo and Frank, who are ready to retire, waiting for the developers' cheque in the mail, Christina is still young, committed to her land and to a grower's way of life. 'I hope to stay in Austral forever. I built my house here. If I have to stop farming, well I don't know. If someone comes and offers me millions, well then, okay. But if that's not the case, I want to stay.'[11]

Driving home, I mentioned to Frances that I had read an article in the previous weekend's newspaper about the few 'protected' market gardens in the Sydney metro area.[12] There are Asian gardens on Occupation Road in Rockdale, which were placed on the state heritage register in 1999. These gardens continue to be worked by growers of Asian vegetables. Frances explained that Occupation Road has survived intact because it is located on swampy land, ill-suited to building. You can't discount its proximity to Sydney Airport, either (so close you fear the choy sum might get grazed by aeroplane tyres). However, Christina, Aldo and Frank won't be as lucky as the Occupation Road growers. Their land is too rich.

*

Luke Harris sees things a little differently, but that's not surprising. Luke is the chief executive officer of Harris Farm, a family-owned and run independent retailer of fruit and vegetables. Luke has spent twelve years at Harris Farm, but has no formal business training. He skipped university and was pearl diving in the Northern Territory when he got a call from his dad, asking him to return home and join the family concern after the sudden death of his grandfather.

Harris Farm prides itself, Luke told me, on selling good quality produce at a good price. 'We have to match the supermarkets,' he said, as we chatted one winter morning over coffee. And Harris Farm has done well, growing to be Australia's largest independent fruit and vegetable retailer with twenty retail sites across New South Wales. They rely

heavily on Christina's fellow growers in places like Lepping-
ton, in Sydney's south-west to supply them with Asian and
other leafy vegetables, herbs, lettuce, Lebanese cucumbers
and so on. This kind of produce does not travel well and is
always much better grown and delivered locally ('Picked at 5
a.m., in the shops by 9 a.m.,' is Luke's mantra).

I asked Luke to nominate the greatest challenge facing
growers. He was resolute that their biggest issue was not
urban sprawl, drought or pressure from retailers, but labour
shortages:

> Growers can't get the workers. Most of the farmers are
> in their sixties, their kids have gone off to university or
> done a real-estate course. They aren't going to take over
> the job. And it is hard to get the truck drivers because
> the traffic is getting worse so it takes them longer to
> truck in the fresh stuff in the morning.

I asked Luke point-blank how the expansion of Sydney is
impacting on growers. 'It's made them very rich. These guys
have come here, worked their arses off and now they are sitting on millions of dollars worth of land.' He acknowledged
that urban sprawl will eventually push out the majority of
market gardeners:

> When the farmers can't say no to the property develop-
> ers because they are offering too much, that's when
> we'll see the market gardens go and the price of vege-
> tables go up. It will be difficult. It will be sad when they
> go and they will go. How long? That's hard to say. If
> they do release more land, then it won't be too long.

Luke recognised that if the gardens are pushed out of the basin and our vegetables have to travel further to get to suburban shops, not only price but also quality will suffer. 'Our stuff in Sydney is very fresh. The irony is you get a lot fresher vegetables in Sydney than you do in places like Orange and Newcastle, even though they are closer to the country. The variety isn't there. It's about good vegetable-growing areas.' Despite all this, Luke is positive about the capacity of his business to deal with higher running costs when market gardens move out of the basin 'We'll be right for the next decade. Decade after that? Who knows?' He might go back to diving for pearls.

*

Many growers feel that only government action can save them now, although it was clear talking to Aldo and Frank that they have given up hope that anything will be done. There is a strong perception that the government and the minister in charge of planning want them out of the growth areas as quickly as possible, and are nonplussed about where (or whether) they will relocate. Getting a statement out of the office of the minister for planning was near impossible. After three emails and three phone calls to his press secretary went unanswered, I gave up. I did, however, manage to get a strong statement from the minister for agriculture:

> Sydney Basin agriculture makes a vital contribution to Sydney's dynamic and evolving food and wine culture. The Sydney Basin has been a melting pot of foods from many cultures beginning with the native foods of the indigenous peoples, followed by the first settlers then

the many cultures from Europe, Asia, the Mediterranean, Americans and now Africa that have arrived on our shores since then.

Sydney's own Hawkesbury Harvest is championing new ways in which local food is being made more accessible directly to consumers through such events as agritourism, farmers' markets, open farm days and a soon to be implemented providore service.

Such initiatives work to ensure that the Sydney Basin continues to generate economic activity associated with its agriculture worth, which is conservatively measured at $2 billion per annum, and continues to employ around 8,000 people.

The last thing we need is concrete and cement from the mountains to the sea.

These are admirable sentiments, but in the absence of any co-ordination with urban planning, the future of market gardens remains bleak. In an arm wrestle between the minister for planning and the minister for agriculture over the future of market gardens, the former will undoubtedly win. The political need to satisfy people's desire for housing is too strong. In the federal election year of 2007, we saw both housing affordability and food prices become political issues; the perception among politicians is that if forced to choose, voters will opt for cheaper housing over cheaper cucumbers and tomatoes.

*

Vegetable gardens are important to migrant Australians. When the first contingents of Italian, Lebanese and Asian migrants arrived, the produce they were accustomed to cooking and eating was not available in Australian stores. Many of these new Australians came from rural areas, where they were used to growing their own fruit and vegetables and raising chickens and goats. These backyard agricultural exploits provided – and continue to provide – migrants with places to reconnect with home, creating 'microcosms of their family holdings in their countries of origin.'[13] This was what my *nonno* did when he first bought a house on Adelaide's North Esplanade, razing the gentile back garden to make way for a huge vegetable patch and rickety shed. Market gardens in Australia have provided successive waves of migrants with a way to make a living. Without language skills or economic resources, they could use the knowledge and capacities they already possessed to earn a little, build businesses and feed their new neighbours in the process.

For Aldo, Frank and Christina, gardening is something more than just a hobby and a source of traditional foodstuffs. It's their career; their gardens are their homes and, if they must sell, their superannuation plans. Running a market garden is undoubtedly hard work – too hard for those who are close to retiring without children willing to take on the business, worn down and worried by increasing costs of all kinds and unable to resist the offers for their land. But what about those who want to stay? The loss of their gardens will hit hard. What other work is available to them if their language skills are poor? Not every child of a market gardener will become a lawyer or an architect. While Christina is paying for her kids to get a good education and a job away from the farm, she told me she would rather they took over the family business than sit around doing nothing. 'Because sometimes there isn't a job,' she pointed out. More than this, for Frances Parker, the rights of those growers who aren't dying to sell up and leave should be respected. 'It's about the rights of small farmers. It's about opportunities and diversity and valuing their contribution to what we eat. That matters.'

From the point of view of food consumers, those of us who don't get the chance to meet and get to know people like Christina and Frank, what would we lose if the market gardens went? Some argue we would hardly notice. Produce would be shipped in overnight from interstate or overseas at little or no increased cost (low labour costs overseas would offset the expense of freight). However, Frances worries about this approach. 'There is this view we can get our food from anywhere in Australia or anywhere around the world. But we don't know what's going to happen with the drought or climate change. We need an insurance policy. We need to protect the good agricultural land we have from urbanisation.' And as another grower, interviewed as part of an ABC radio documentary on market gardens, commented, the issue of quality shouldn't be flippantly dismissed. 'Where is Sydney going to get its fresh produce from? It will have to be trucked in from elsewhere. They really should be harvested and eaten fresh not sitting in a truck.'[14]

At a time when drought is raising food prices, when rural farmers are struggling, when the cost (financial and environmental) of transport is escalating, it seems crazy that we are planning our cities without food security in mind. Consumers are increasingly aware of where their food is coming from and often expressing a desire to support Australian growers.[15] Food security should be a factor in any government's strategy for creating a sustainable and livable city. It is as important a concern as transport, infrastructure and decent housing. Such a strategy would go beyond heritage listing old market gardens. It might include creating special peri-urban farming zones and capping residential development. We should care more about the pressures facing growers in the Sydney Basin as well as those still farming around the urban perimeters of Australia's other major cities. We hear so much about the plight of the rural farming community – why doesn't our concern extend to peri-urban farmers such as Christina? These workers are part of an industry that provides us with the foods nutritionists constantly tell us are essential to a healthy lifestyle. Once the gardens are gone and the houses and highways built, it will be too late to complain about the cost and quality of lettuce.

BASIC MEALS FOR THE

ULTRA RICH

I buy organic garlic. It's more expensive, of course, than the perfectly formed, pure white bulbs of Chinese garlic. At my local supermarket it costs 98 cents for a four pack of regular garlic versus $5.99 for two of the organic variety. I buy organic garlic for a couple of reasons. It's juicy and sweet with a powerful flavour. It makes me feel virtuous, too. I imagine the hardworking farmer, shunning the use of harmful chemicals, whose crop I am helping support. But I must admit that the main reason I buy organic garlic is because, well, size matters. The bulbs are enormous. I only have to peel and slice one clove for use in a dish, as opposed to having to fiddle with four or more of the tiny Chinese ones. In my case, buying organic is a far more selfish choice than it might at first appear.

Eric Love appreciates this. As the deputy chair of the Organic Federation of Australia, he spends a lot of his time thinking about why people buy (or don't buy) organic food.[1] I approached Eric for an interview so I could understand how the organic food movement was progressing in Australia. What were the significant barriers to its growth? Eric works in a tiny office, not much larger than my bedroom, sharing the space with four colleagues. Not the best venue for an interview, so he suggested going out for coffee. He surprised me when he said we should head off to a Starbucks-like coffee shop, not a particularly good one, that didn't even offer organic coffee. Clearly Eric was not a purist, I thought. Reclining in comfy chairs to the strains of bad eighties music, Eric began by telling me something of the history of organics in Australia. 'The organic sector really started here in 1984. The OFA was formed out of a need for a more formalised approach to organic growing.' The early 1980s was a time of increased awareness about food safety and environmental issues, in Australia but more so overseas. American TV ads featured actor Meryl Streep asking President Bush senior why she had to wash her broccoli in detergent before she cooked it.

As the years passed, the organics movement developed faster in the United Kingdom and Europe than in Australia. The main reason for this, in Eric's opinion, was food safety. 'In those other countries there have been real food scares, whereas in Australia there has been the perception amongst consumers that our produce is reasonably safe and nutritious.' Certainly the working mothers I had interviewed in Brisbane agreed; Michelle told me she never bought organic because she had no problem with conventional produce: 'I am happy with the fruit and veg we buy. Sometimes I don't even wash it! I am confident it is safe.' Even without the spur of food-safety scares, Eric reported, the organics movement is growing in Australia at about 30 to 50 per cent every year, according to the OFA's research. Marketing journalist Julian Lee reports in his book *How Good Are You?* that between 1995 and 2005, the retail organics sector grew from $25 million dollars to around $500 million dollars.[2] This substantial growth, however, is from a very low base; organics constitutes around 1 per cent of retail sales.[3]

I decided to fire a few generally held beliefs about organic foods at Eric to see if they were accurate. The first was cost. Organic food is seen as more expensive than non-organic food. The introduction of organic fruit and vegetables to supermarkets works to reinforce this belief in the minds of grocery buyers. Organics in Coles and Woolworths are packaged differently, tucked away in a special part of the fresh food section, like VIPs roped off from the rest of the hoi polloi at a nightclub. However, Eric told me that consumer support for organic food 'cuts across demographic boundaries.' 'You would think it would be only the super-rich that buy organic, but that's not the case.' That's because, as Eric explained, most consumers take a cherry-picking approach to organic food. They might buy organic lettuce, chicken and baby food but stop short of ensuring their entire trolley is certified organic. In Eric's view, the latter option would certainly strain the financial resources of even a comfortably middle-class family. 'Can people go 100 per cent organic? They probably could but they would have to be pretty wealthy to do so.'

I wanted to test this theory about the cost of organic. So I ventured out on one of my shopping tests. Take a 'typical' family meal: crumbed chicken schnitzels with salad on wholemeal rolls with roasted potato wedges, with fruit and ice cream for dessert. Compare the following dockets for the ingredients, one from an organic supermarket and the other from a conventional supermarket.[4] We would expect the organic food to cost more, but just how much more?

Organic	*Conventional*
Bananas $2.99 per kilogram	Bananas $2.48 per kilogram
Raspberries $11.99 punnet	Raspberries $5.98 punnet
Strawberries $7.95 punnet	Strawberries $6.98 punnet
Avocado $3.95 each	Avocado $1.18 each
Butter lettuce $2.50 each	Butter lettuce $1.48 each
One dozen eggs $8.95	One dozen free-range eggs $5.67
Two chicken breasts $14.98	Two free-range chicken breasts $9.01
300 grams bread crumbs $4.20	300 grams bread crumbs $2.10
Six spelt wholemeal rolls $6.35	Six wholemeal rolls $1.19
Tomatoes $7.95 per kilogram	Tomatoes $5.78 per kilogram
Cookies and cream ice-cream $10.95	Cookies and cream ice-cream $7.25
Unwashed potatoes $3.95	Unwashed potatoes $2.98
TOTAL $86.71	TOTAL $52.08

As journalist Michael Harden comments, organic-food activists argue that:

> The extra money you pay for organic produce brings the price closer to the real value of producing food. It is even argued that the price you pay is something of a bargain if weighed against costs to health and the environmental damage caused by much conventional farming.[5]

This 'pay now or pay later' argument should be more persuasive to people who can afford to pay now. Of course, there are families for whom a thirty-dollar increase in the weekly food bill is a significant difference. Then there is the issue of taste. As Patricia, one of the Brisbane mums, commented, she and her family can't taste the difference between organic and conventional and therefore can't justify the extra cost. Then there is the question of appearance. Luke Harris, the chief operating officer of Harris Farm, told me their excursions into producing and selling organic food in their retail outlets had been a mixed success. 'We try every year. But you put an expensive, limp little organic cauliflower next to a large, snowy white normal one, well the consumer can't help but choose the good looking one.' The organics movement faces a real marketing challenge if the majority of consumers are unconvinced that organic food tastes better or is better for you than the conventional variety.

What about the distribution of organic food? There is a perception that organic food stores are clustered in inner-city suburbs and regional areas with a hippy bent like Byron Bay or the Blue Mountains. Eric doesn't entirely agree with that analysis. 'There is a different method of distribution involved. In the city you might have places like Macro [Wholefoods, Australia's most successful organic supermarket chain] in urban areas and particular suburbs, whereas organics are distributed in regional areas via farmers' markets. And they may not even be labelled "organic" in that context.' And of course, there is the informal, domestic organics movement, people who might grow their own in their backyards without the use of pesticides or intensive farming.[6] Still, Macro only maintains its outlets in relatively prosperous suburbs, like Bondi Junction and Crows Nest in Sydney and Armadale and Richmond in Melbourne. Macro is planning to extend its reach to the northern and western suburbs of Sydney and

Melbourne, and to regional areas such as Geelong, New-castle and Bowral.[7] Not that you can blame them for opening stores only where there is a market for what they sell, where people can afford to buy organic and are already committed to the principle.

Which brought me to another thorny question: is organic food a political movement or a business proposition? Eric acknowledged that the tension between altruism and self-interest, between the true believers and the bean counters, is a major challenge for the continued growth of the sector:

> The business of organic foods grew out of the environ-mental movement. That's both its strength and its weak-ness. In the beginning there wasn't a lot of attention to meeting consumer needs. There was this attitude that 'we are the organic movement and if people don't like it then tough.'

Eric felt that this attitude was shifting but the tension remains, exacerbated by developments in the industry such as the big end of town – Coles and Woolworths – 'dipping their toes into the organic market.'[8] In 2004, Coles was the first large retailer to introduce its own brand of organic products, including orange juice, milk, pasta and canned tomatoes.[9] What was the response from the true believers? 'Mixed,' Eric admitted. 'Supermarkets haven't had a good reputation for looking after producers in the past. We have responded to that by having a fair-trade policy. My observation is that they are doing well.'

The emergence of big business in the organics market is one sign that the industry is at a crossroads, confronting the challenges of further commercialisation as well as the question of accreditation.[10] 'We are on the cusp of huge changes in the organic sector,' Eric said. He hopes the next decade will see more self-sufficiency, less reliance on imported products and diversification in the domestic production of organics. This, he believes, will boost the affordability, variety and convenience of organics generally. All this has to happen without the values of the industry being compromised by commercialisation. On this point, Eric comes across more as a pragmatist than as an ideologue. 'If it's not commercially viable, none of the necessary improvements will happen.'

In her research on ethical consumption, academic Hélène Cherrier conducted extensive interviews with nine people who had made the switch to buying organic food. She found that for all nine, the trigger for this change was 'an uncontrollable or unpredictable life event' that threatened their sense of personal safety, such as a serious illness or watching a shocking event on television. This event made them more aware of their surroundings and the fragility of life. Choosing to become an ethical consumer is part of a broader project of transformation into 'the kind of person one should aspire to be.'[11] If the growth of the organics movement depends on every citizen experiencing a traumatic life event, then expansion will be slow. However, it may not come to that. Interestingly, it seems that one of the groups most supportive of organic foods is young families. 'Baby foods are huge,' Eric told me. 'It's one of the largest selling lines of organic foods.' Business manager for Heinz, Seang Lee, echoed Eric's comments in an interview with *B&T News*. 'In baby food, organic is much bigger because of health concerns and people are willing to pay more.'[12] No surprise there. What with growing parental concern about children's allergies and food intolerances, it's no shock that organics has made easy headway into the children's food market. I have spotted more than a couple of mums at the checkout with their toddlers, trolleys full of non-organic products, but baby food all certified.[13] This leads me back to the point I made at the beginning of this chapter about the 'selfishness' of consumers when it comes to food. There has to be something in it for them – taste, quality, nutritional content, time savings, health benefits. As Eric explained to me, 'People are receptive to paying more if they are getting a definite benefit from organics.'

There is a term used in the organics industry to describe a business that has embarked on the three-year process to become 'certified': organic in conversion. Eric tells me it's an easier process than you might think. Once certified, producers can use the term when marketing their product. The conversion process for most consumers will undoubtedly be a much slower process, hampered by price, place and perception. For now, the organics movement can rely on a few stalwarts – the worried parents, the committed greenies and another culturally influential group: the Bobos.

*

At least one Saturday a month, I find myself walking the aisles of a growers' market in a posh area of my city, about ten minutes' drive from where I live. It's a place where people with lots of money and time on their hands do a spot of recreational food shopping. Most of the fresh produce sold there is organic – fruit, veggies and meat. No chicken is harmed in the making of this market; all eggs and drumsticks are cruelty-free. Some of the stuff on sale, such as the cheeses and small goods, are imported from picturesque towns in Italy and France. Convenience is not a priority. There are few one-stop shops. It's all about specialisation. There is a stall dedicated to strawberries, one selling a wide variety of olives, another devoted to salmon, next door to a woman selling only lettuce and tomatoes. There are a number of people selling bread; correction, a number of 'artisan bakers.' For a relatively small market, there are two coffee stalls with long queues. I usually take the one with the shortest wait, selling free-trade organic coffee. My regular order is a latte, which serves a dual purpose. I can get my caffeine hit while assisting the people of East Timor to rebuild their economy.

The providores at this farmers' market are a mixed bunch. Some would fit in to the larger markets in Chinatown or out west. Others would look more at home in a gourmet deli or café. The buyers at this market are variations on a theme. Good-looking young parents with kids in Bugaboo prams and trendy clothes, snacking on well decorated cupcakes. Older couples debate whether to buy lilies or tulips for the front entrance. The other noticeable fact about the market is that there is scarcely a plastic bag to be seen. Green bags, French baskets, trolleys and the occasional prestige stroller are the carry-alls popular with this crowd. On an average trip, my own green bag might contain the following contents:

Bag of organic apples	$5
Bag of organic zucchini	$6
Olive bread	$6.50
500g organic, free-trade coffee	$11.50

Two organic lamb shanks	$8.00
Bag of organic lettuce	$3
Flowers	$33

EQUALS: Sucker prepared to spend a lot of money on not a lot of food

Farmers' markets like this are undoubtedly middle-class spaces, trading not simply in lovely produce, but also in the values of authenticity, simplicity and heritage.[14] By shopping here, market-goers are attempting a return to a world of personal and intimate communication between neighbours and friends, buyers and sellers, people and things. It's like a mini-break from the banal consumption we might experience in the more usual places we shop for food: the convenience store, the shopping centre and the supermarket.

My description of this farmers' market is derisory, but I must admit that in many ways, these are my people. I come here as often as I can when time permits. I love it because I am what *New York Times* columnist David Brooks calls a 'Bobo,' and this is how Bobos eat.

*

It all started in the 1980s, that decade notorious for its economic revolutions and perplexing shifts in the axes of politics and culture. It was a time, according to Michael Symons, when 'many yuppies became gourmands.'[15] Popular culture reflected this embrace of foodism by society's elite. In Oliver Stone's movie *Wall Street*, set in the mid eighties, trader Bud Fox hooks up with interior designer Darian (played by the cyborg-like Darryl Hannah). They cement their new relationship with an elaborate cooking spree – handmade sushi,

fresh pasta, gourmet ice-cream and a wealth of other personally crafted treats. Once the grub is all laid out in front of
them on their $15,000 dining table, Bud says, 'Let's not even
eat. Let's just watch it.' Food as status symbol, like a bespoke
watch or handmade attaché case.

It was in this avaricious decade, according to David Brooks,
that the Bobo was conceived. The Bobo is the unlikely love-
child of the 1960s and the 1980s, a hybrid character whose
activities and values span 'the bourgeois realm of ambition
and worldly success' and 'the bohemian world of creativity.'[16]
He is the 'stockbroker with hippy tastes,' the corporate lawyer
with a penchant for rock climbing and African drumming,
the IT entrepreneur who always eats organic and vegetarian.[17]
In Brooks' book *Bobos in Paradise*, the world of food is an in-
finitely expressive site for the articulation of the Bobo philosophy. Consider the following description of the food choices
in the small, Bobo-style town of Wayne, Pennsylvania:

> Once an espresso desert, [Wayne] now has six gourmet
> coffee-houses … There are several new food places in
> town [selling] gourmet jelly beans, spiced apple cider
> sorbet and gelato in such flavours as Zuppa Inglese.
> There are now two stores that specialize in discriminat-
> ing picnic baskets … For lunch, Your Gourmet Kitchen
> sells crab Panini and herb-grilled chicken breasts with
> sprouts on sourdough … The Great Harvest Bread
> Company … sells apricot almond or spinach feta loaf
> for $4.75 a pop … As you walk in the door … a short
> lecture commences on the naturalness of the ingredi-
> ents and the authenticity of the baking process, which,
> in fact, is being carried out right there in front of you …

The visitor to Fresh Fields [supermarket] is confronted with a big sign that says 'Organic items today: 130.' This is like a barometer of virtue ... Customers can stroll amidst the radish sprouts, bins of brown and basmati rice ... and the vegetarian dog biscuits, basking in their reflected wholesomeness.[18]

The Bobo food world is one of eating tours of multicultural suburbs and 'unspoilt' corners of Asia and Europe. Ordinary supermarkets are shunned by the Bobo in favour of organic stores, specialty shops and farmers' markets. Bobo restaurants run the gamut from humble but authentic noodle bars to mega-expensive establishments that offer nothing but a dégustation menu matched with appropriate wines. The Bobo kitchen is well decked out, the playground for their favourite competitive sport – the dinner party. The Bobo food world is well represented in the cookbooks and magazines that stock the shelves and cabinets of any tastefully renovated Bobo house.

We usually associate food for the wealthy and well connected in our society with *haute cuisine* of the kind served in the grand restaurants and hotels of Europe.[19] This is food that is refined and elegant, elaborately prepared and presented, highly processed, featuring sauces that have been puréed, strained, reduced and reduced again over long periods of time. In essence, food that has been endlessly fiddled with; it is known as 'vanguard cuisine' or 'techno-emotional cuisine' by those in the know. Today, the menu served at the world-renowned El Bulli restaurant in Spain exemplifies this style; sculpture meets science, with a jus or a sauce applied with a syringe or frozen by dry ice.[20]

Bobos might eat this kind of food every now and then, for an anniversary meal or business lunch. But it's not their cuisine of choice. Bobos favour eating that has a certain 'peasant aesthetic.' They prize food that is rustic, handmade, artisan-crafted, stripped down to its bare essentials, unadulterated and authentic. In Brooks' view, the upper-class preference for the smooth and the refined has now shifted to mimic the formerly working-class necessity for the simple, almost bucolic. 'Everything the old gentry tried to make smooth, we in today's educated gentry try to make rough,' as Brooks explains.[21] When renovating their dwellings, Bobos pull up carpets to expose ancient floorboards or strip off wallpaper to reveal plain plastered walls or brick. They convert old warehouses, workers' cottages or loft apartments into expensive, 'shabby chic' versions of their former shabby selves. When it comes to food, the same principles apply. Simple ingredients and traditional methods are prized. Even better if the produce retains a roughness or imperfection, the dirt or leaves still clinging to the skin or stalk. This is privilege cloaked in the garb of poverty. 'The beauty of such a strategy,' argues Brooks, 'is that it allows us to be egalitarian and pretentious at the same time.'[22]

For Bobos, the best places to shop for food – farmers' markets, specialty stores, organic co-operatives and the like – incorporate this fetish for the rustic. As cultural studies academic Jean Duruz points out, food tourism (a favourite Bobo pastime) is dominated by 'the urban, imaginary nostalgia for a seemingly coherent, uncomplicated "other" Australia,' one in which farmers' wives dish out tasty, country cooking (jams, stews, pies and crumbles) made with those pure ingredients nurtured by her husband. (Of course, nostalgia is always selective, Duruz argues; it forgets the harshness of farm life past and present.)[23] Even places like the David Jones Food Hall combine supermarket convenience with specialist stalls and knowledgeable shop attendants, imitating the markets and neighbourhood food strips that Bobos venerate.[24] These places stand in stark contrast to the suburban, the industrial, the bulk-sized, one-size-fits-all food world of the bog-standard plebeian supermarket. In the eyes of any dedicated Bobo foodie, this kind of supermarket is villainous, as the following passage from Symons' *One Continuous Picnic* illustrates:

> Good food has never come from factory farms, process lines, canteens, supermarkets and fast-food chains. It still belongs to careful vegetable gardens, painstaking cheese-makers and dedicated chef-patrons, meeting in the bustling market place. Good food comes from 'smiling vineyards' and lunch on verandahs. So, when we enjoy a healthy diet of fresh, local produce treated with proper respect, when we learn from peasants … we have at last found a national cuisine, cultivated a continent.[25]

On the face of it, this appears a modest task – eating healthy, fresh, local produce. And yet, as this book has shown, most Australians in today's 'peasant' class struggle to do so. Simple food of the kind Symons envisages is not a staple of everyday life, but a luxury product. As a 2006 Ipsos Mackay Report on luxury goods found, simplicity and restraint have acquired a new cachet, as a reaction to the conspicuous consumption of the mass market. 'Some affluent consumers have responded to the appeal of "reverse snobbery" or to the growing sense in the community that we are rushing too quickly to enjoy life's "simple pleasures" – especially food, travel and time together.'[26] In today's luxury market, the most attractive products are those that appear more humble and authentic, like pasta made with traditional methods using vintage Italian implements. According to the Bobo worldview, only 'vulgarians' lavish money on ostentatious jewellery and accoutrements for the home. The cultivated 'restrict their lavish spending to necessities,' such as artisan breads, homemade jams and the like.[27] Blessed be the cheese-makers.

Bobo food is not just about 'authenticity' and the pursuit of a romanticised peasant aesthetic. It is also about 'value.' Not value for money (no, never that), but 'values.' For the Bobo, it's not enough for food to taste good, to be organic and hand-crafted and so forth. Food must mean something. It must *do* something other than provide nourishment. According to Brooks, it is typical of the Bobo philosophy that mundane, everyday tasks, such as food shopping, should be socially useful and meaningful:

> Marx once wrote that the bourgeois take all that is sacred and make it profane. The Bobos take everything that is profane and make it sacred. We have taken something that might have been grubby and materialistic and turned it into something elevated. We take the quintessential bourgeois activity, shopping, and turn it into a quintessential bohemian activity: art, philosophy, social action. Bobos possess the Midas touch in reverse. Everything we handle turns into soul.[28]

In the Bobo world, the three o'clock munchies become an exercise in social and political conviction. A few years ago, I was searching the aisles of a health-food store close to my office for a moderately healthy snack to combat my usual mid-afternoon slump. I found an apricot and almond bar within my price range. I turned it over to investigate the fat and sugar content. Under the nutritional info, I found the following declaration: *Five per cent of profits from the sale of this product go to helping achieve peace in the Middle East.*

That's a lot of pressure to put on confectionary. I was intrigued by this muesli-bar mission statement and went back to the office to look at the manufacturer's website, www.peaceworks.com. I discovered that the snack bar's producer was a not-*only*-for-profit company that combines the making of gourmet foods with conflict resolution. Here's a quote from their website:

> PeaceWorks have proven that we can build and sustain a profitable company AND do a little good in the world. Together with people striving to co-exist, we create and deliver unique and exciting specialty foods – only the freshest ingredients, always all-natural, always delicious. PeaceWorks currently does business with Israelis, Palestinians, Egyptians, South Africans, Turks, Indonesians and Sri Lankans.
>
> PeaceWorks unites people on opposite sides of a conflict via a shared goal – manufacturing a pesto or a spice mix. Other than the apricot and almond bar, PeaceWorks do a line of tapenades and pestos produced in Israel through mutual co-operation between Israelis and Arabs. The olives are grown in Palestinian

EATING BETWEEN THE LINES

villages, the glass jars are made in Egypt, and the sun-dried tomatoes come from Turkey. I have a jar of the stuff in my fridge. Called 'Moshe and Ali's Sun-dried Tomato Sprate,' the label has cartoon images of an Arab and a Jew smiling and winking, seemingly full of Semitic love.

In the shop where I purchased the PeaceWorks muesli bar there are examples in every aisle and on every shelf of food products doing their bit for the environment, charities, world peace and community development. There are lemon biscuits that help regenerate and protect the British countryside and wildlife. The profits of ginger snaps are donated to a charitable foundation working with disadvantaged youth. I can eat these with a cup of fair-trade tea or coffee. When it comes to chocolate, I have a choice. Do I want the dark chocolate with hazelnut toffee that saves the endangered rhinos or plain milk chocolate that assists a co-operative in Ghana? It's a tough call, but in the end the earnest picture of the rhino and the supposed antioxidants in dark chocolate will sway me. I am glad to see that one of the honeys I can purchase is made in hives that are constructed from environmentally friendly materials. For a more substantial meal, I can have jasmine rice that assists a co-operative in Thailand, matched with red salmon that is, of course, dolphin friendly.

It's easy to mock the Bobo food world, even from within. It seems to confirm all the well-circulated stereotypes about chardonnay socialists and the café latte set, with their rarefied tastes and slavish devotion to the latest trendy political cause.

But Bobo food – whether it be organic, free-trade, hand-made or artisan crafted – is a wonderful way to eat. Nourishing for the body and soul. Pity so few of us get to enjoy such a menu every day.

CONCLUSION: REPUBLIC
OF FOOD

Republic: a state open to all citizens without any distinction as to race, colour, creed or sex.
Food: something that nourishes or sustains.

Food is rich in meaning. It reflects our values and our identity. It mirrors social trends and shifting behaviours. And so we look at eating to better understand the eater. At a time when social class seems increasingly difficult to define, eating habits can be a useful means of describing social distinctions. For their book *Ordinary People's Politics*, political scientists Judith Brett and Anthony Moran interviewed Lois Angus, a public sector clerk in her sixties. They asked Lois about her own social status and the different social groups that exist in Australian society. Rather than referring to categories of class or race or nationality, Lois classified herself and others easily through food:

> You have society people who have big banquets and dinners and entertain in big numbers. Then you get the middle-of-the-road person who goes out with two or three friends to a reasonably priced restaurant ... Then you get people who like to go to parties ... Then there

are the more family people who have barbecues …
There's a group of people who go out every second night
and buy take-away, McDonald's or whatever, just to
save cooking. I don't fit in with that type. I like a basic
home-cooked meal. I like to eat in good restaurants …
If that makes me a little bit middle of the road, that's
where I am.[1]

If food can reflect social status, it can also reflect social
inequality. Throughout this book I have shown how three
elements – money, time and place – work together in complex ways to shape the diet of Australians. Those on low
incomes are clearly the most hamstrung, but there are others
who are similarly disadvantaged, namely people who are
time-poor and whose living and working arrangements distance them from quality, affordable food. When these three
elements combine, the effects can be disastrous.

There was one particular moment during the research for
this book that crystallised my thinking about food and inequality. I was visiting a factory in Sydney's outer northern
suburbs. The factory floor was the usual cacophony of industrial noise and human movement. Chemical smells pene-
trated everything. The workers were all, without exception,
from migrant backgrounds; Asian and Pacific Islanders
dominated the group. As we neared the end of the tour I
spotted a vending machine near the exit, half full of the
usual assortment of chocolate and chips. Stuck to its front
was a large, handwritten sign on grubby white cardboard. It
said: 'We depend on this machine for breakfast. It's broken
AGAIN. Please fix it.' I was taken aback. How could it be
that Twisties were all these workers could depend on for

'the most important meal of the day'? Then I thought through the logistics. Many of these factory employees may well struggle to afford to live in the large high-rent houses that exist close to their employment. Perhaps they have to travel for long periods to get to work. Maybe, like many Australians, they have little or no time in the morning to eat breakfast and maybe, on their way to work, there are few available places to stop and buy anything healthy. And of course, a chocolate bar only costs a few dollars, compared with a takeaway yoghurt and fruit salad or raisin toast at a café. Time pressures, travel issues and the cost of food combine to create a situation in which a Snickers bar is the most dependable form of breakfast. In contrast, at my workplace, there is an abundance of healthy cereals, a selection of fruit, bread for toast, spreads of all kinds, rice crackers and biscuits. Even if I fail to pick up breakfast at the many cafés open for business on my way to work, I can always fall back on what my employer provides.

Lack of time and lack of money may be the most obvious explanations for these workers' dependence on the vending machine, but there must also be other, less quantifiable, factors at play. If we feel time-poor, do we turn to fast food because we assume it must be the cheapest and quickest option, even when a few slices of toast at home might be just as quick and just as cheap? What role is played by the force of habit, or by the sense that we don't deserve better food than this? My food tour through Australia has taught me that our relationship with food is always complex and changing; there is rarely one simple cause or one simple solution to the food challenges we face.

Looking at how Australians eat, I wonder whether we are

headed towards a culture of extremes, of very rich and very poor, of thin and obese, of Mars Bar munchers and pesto puritans. We have long known about the extremes of wealth and poverty in developing countries. And yet now it seems that, as Raj Patel argues, even in developing countries 'the contradictions of obesity, hunger, poverty and wealth are becoming more acute.'[2] At a time of extraordinary and extended economic prosperity in Australia, economic disadvantage remains stubbornly entrenched. Its existence is masked, perhaps, by the constant chatter in media, political and business circles about the resources boom, low unemployment, high GDP and record retail spending. Throughout the last decade of economic good news, religious and social services organisations have continued to direct our attention to the fact that intergenerational disadvantage exists and is concentrated in certain sections of the population.[3] There is certainly a strong public perception that the gap between rich and poor in our society is widening.[4] And while academics and statisticians have clashed over exactly how many Australians can be considered 'poor' and where we should set the official poverty line, a 2004 Senate committee report found that poverty in Australia increased from 10.2 per cent to 16.7 per cent between 1972 and 1990. In 2000 it was found that around one in eight children in Australia was living in poverty, a high rate when compared with most other industralised countries.[5] Recent research by the Social Policy Research Centre at the University of New South Wales showed that in 2004 anywhere between 9.9 per cent to 19.8 per cent of Australians were living in poverty.[6] The Senate report found that relative poverty was high among single-parent families, unemployed people, immigrants from

Oceania, the Americas and Asia, indigenous Australians and families with children.[7] These are the very groups that we know to be at the highest risk of overweight, obesity and diet-related illness.

Of course, this new culture of extremes does not only apply to questions of income and the distribution of economic resources. There are the growing extremes now associated with place in our society. In conjunction with the longstanding divide between city and country, we have postcodes of poverty within booming and affluent cities and towns. This is increasingly a divide between the centre and the periphery, exacerbated by housing prices, transport difficulties and employment opportunities. Then there is the impact of time (or lack of it) on our diet and eating habits. There is a good reason why the term 'time-poor' has such contemporary resonance. Many Australian workers are coping with the challenges of balancing work and family commitments, with particular pressures on those juggling shiftwork and multiple jobs. We know Australians work longer hours and perform more unpaid overtime than their colleagues in other equivalent countries.[8] All this overwork can have serious physical side effects. As Dorothy Broom and others have found, while unemployment is rightly associated with poor health, some jobs – with high stress, long hours and bad working conditions – may actually be worse than no job at all.[9] Indeed, in 2003 the Australian Institute of Health and Welfare reported that Australians who were employed were more likely to be overweight than those who were not in the labour force.[10] In part, this must be a consequence of the impact of long hours on the capacity of workers to plan, shop, prepare and eat healthy food on a regular basis.

It's not just the sheer lack of time that affects our approach to food and cooking. As Margaret Visser argues, the social and psychological impact of our accelerated culture can be just as damaging to our diets:

> Feeling rushed is ... an important component of our economy; it causes people to buy more, pay more, try more things and more means to compensate for the stress, or at least to alleviate the anxiety. It also makes us work harder and longer – and therefore leave ourselves less time ... We eat out or buy ready-prepared food to eat at home in order to save time, but also – and more insidiously – because we feel we have no time to do otherwise. Many of us never really learn to cook, and therefore cooking remains not only time-consuming but unrewarding.[11]

Time has become the most sought-after luxury product.[12] Those with the time, not to mention the money and opportunity, to shop in Bobo style can enjoy a wonderfully healthy and diverse diet, the best Australian food culture has to offer. For the time-poor, the income-poor and the postcode-poor, this kind of food is the stuff of TV cooking shows and gourmet magazines. It may entice and entertain but, as food writer Alan Saunders puts it, it is about as relevant to their world as 'amateur poets are to the pop charts.'[13]

*

I started this book with a working theory that eating and cooking habits reflect the various strains of inequality in Australia – between men and women, rich and poor, host and migrant, indigenous and non-indigenous, country and city. In the process of writing, I uncovered more than just depressing facts about diabetes in indigenous communities or the concentration of fast-food outlets in socially disadvantaged suburbs. I remain cheered, even amazed, by many things. For example, that working mums like the ones I met in Brisbane still manage to find a way to cook healthy meals for their families, day after day. This, despite the fact it would be easier and perhaps even cheaper to rely on take-away or processed foods. I am also pleased to have discovered some small, very small, signs that men, particularly the next generation of boys, might be more interested in cooking beyond turning snags on a barbecue. I witnessed first-hand the potential that food has to forge meaningful connections between previously antipathetic migrant groups. That the simple act of sharing lunch can initiate a conversation between people from different cultures and different generations. And then there were all the people I met as I researched this book. Like Norma, who is trying to improve the food habits of the indigenous community; Christina, fighting to hold on to her market garden and way of life; Frances and her dogged campaign to ensure her city isn't engulfed by concrete from the mountains to the sea; and Leila, who has put aside personal unhappiness to start cooking healthy meals for one. While hardcore foodies lament the decline of cooking skills, the rise of the supermarket and the dominance of pre-prepared foods (albeit at the same time rhapsodising about our wonderful food culture), I see things differently. There is good news and bad news, but not of the kind we anticipate.

The burgeoning ranks of celebrity chefs and the explosion of food media have been a boon for our publishing and gasto-tourism industries, but hasn't exactly brought good food and eating to the vast majority. The exception here is Jamie Oliver, who said in his *Good Housekeeping* interview that: 'I don't want a country of gastronomes, but I do want a country of kids who can go to uni knowing how to make spag bol and a half-decent salad.' Rather than trying to impress the food establishment, Oliver's mission is, as Blythman describes, 'to broaden the food knowledge and cooking capability of a great mass of ordinary people.'[14] Jamie aside, it would be naive to rely on celebrity chefs to be the driving force in any democratisation of good eating.

Nostalgic calls for a return to the past (evident in so much commentary about the decline of domestic cooking standards, the demise of the family dinner and the eating habits of singles) are of little help either. None of the social shifts that have precipitated these changes, particularly in regard to the working lives of women, are about to change any time soon.

Blaming individuals for their own bad eating habits and food choices is also unhelpful, as is shaming parents for their children's weight issues. Strategies such as fat camps and humiliating school weigh-ins are up there with TV shows like *The Biggest Loser* and *Honey, We're Killing the Kids*, feeding into what writer Anne Manne describes as a culture of ritual humiliation and group aggression.[15] Not the best basis for an effective public health strategy.

What about 'the silver bullet,' education? Certainly improved education in schools about cooking and nutrition is important, as are public health campaigns about food and nutrition aimed at adults. There is evidence that vital information about food and eating isn't getting through to particular communities with specific education and language

problems; indigenous communities and newly arrived Sudanese communities were two examples that came up in the
research for this book. And yet, I worry that 'more education'
is a trap in itself. If we educate and still people don't change
their eating habits, we can easily fall back to the 'blame and
shame the individual' approach. There is more food and diet
information available now than ever before – wrapped around
every can and packet, broadcast by every possible media, lin-
ing the shelves of large sections of large bookstores. And yet
even the most sober analysts recognise that overweight and
obesity rates are increasing at the very time that the body of
information about food and diet is expanding. As the World
Health Organisation stated in 1998, 'Access to good, affordable food makes more difference to what people eat than
health education.'[16]

In 2007, food got political. The last time we saw food
become a central part of the national political discussion was
when the GST became an issue in the federal elections of
1993 and 1998. For the Labor Party in particular, a tax on
milk and bread seemed manifestly unfair. In 1993, Labor
campaigned heavily on these grounds. In an election in
which the women's vote was deemed crucial to victory, Labor
reminded grocery buyers that the GST would cost them
every time they hired a video, ordered a pizza or did the
weekly shopping. When the GST question was resurrected
in the late 1990s, parliamentarians spent question time quiz-
zing each other about the cost of soup. A Democrat-enforced
compromise was reached and the GST became law in mid
2000, with 'fresh' food exempt from the new consumption
tax. This has led to a strange scenario: a roast chicken attracts
GST but a kilo of flour is GST-free. How often does a busy

working mum rely on the former for a midweek dinner, and how often does she need the latter to bake her own bread?

In 2007, with the GST debates a distant memory, the conversation was all about food prices. Consumers were noticing that grocery prices were rising, at the very time they were paying more for petrol and housing. The big supermarkets were blamed and Labor promised an inquiry into food prices. Consumers were also making the link between rising food costs and rising temperatures. There were consistent media reports that the drought and the water crisis would continue to drive up the prices of dairy, meat, fruit and vegetables.[17] Blaming government, particularly the federal government, for its lack of action on drought and water (and by association climate change) seemed like the way to go for many voters.[18]

Since the election of the federal Labor government in late 2007, food has become even more political. At the 2020 Vision Conference in early 2008, a number of ideas were proposed to combat obesity. These included taxes on junk food, the establishment of a national preventative health agency, the delivery of fresh fruit and vegetables to primary schools and to indigenous communities, a new food labelling system using a simple 'traffic light' system of colour coding, and a ban on the marketing of junk-food to children.[19]

Although some of these ideas are good ones, they tend to focus on information and education. Where are the practical initiatives to address the deeper inequalities that prevent some Australians from accessing healthy, affordable food? To effectively address these issues, we need a new politics of food in this country. This could, and should, embrace the issues of genetically modified foods, animal cruelty, food additives (including hormones) and misleading labelling and advertising. It might include a heightened awareness of the environmental impact of what we eat. We might see the introduction, as in the United Kingdom, of 'green labelling' on products. This would go beyond the idea of food miles, to show the total greenhouse-gas emissions created in the production, transport and eventual disposal of certain foods.[20] Similarly, we may well see the introduction of a 'watermark' on certain products, reflecting the amount of water used in various manufacturing processes. These kinds of developments would enhance the potential for consumer activism, offering people an opportunity to reject companies that squander our natural resources and to support those that don't.

At its most effective, a new food politics would attempt to fulfil the mission and values of the Slow Food movement. Founded in Italy by Carlo Petrini, the Slow Food movement's aims are local and global, practical and ambitious. Its credo is that food must be 'good, clean and fair.' Good, because food should always be of high quality; clean because our food should be produced in a way that doesn't put ecosystems under strain, ruin the environment or destroy biodiversity; and fair, because workers in the food industries should be paid a decent wage, local food production should be supported and protected and all consumers, regardless of social class, should be able to afford good quality food.[21] In Australia, the Slow Food movement has been small and on the whole has lacked much of a political bent. Judging from their newsletters and websites, Slow Food in Australia is largely focused on food fairs and workshops, gastronomic and cultural tours, cooking demonstrations and corporate programs.[22] A Bobo's heaven, but hardly the revolution advocated by Petrini. To be truly revolutionary, the Slow Food movement needs to look beyond artisan-crafted goat's cheese and address the needs of the most disadvantaged. A movement truly committed to achieving universal access to better food would champion the cause of peri-urban farmers, lobby for better access to fresh food in remote indigenous communities, and work to improve the standard of eating in suburbs such as Munno Para.

'Green' labelling, consumer boycotts, social movements organised around the principles of slow, local and organic, will all have a part to play in this possible politics of food. But, as public policy academics Barnett *et al* assert, 'real change to the way we eat will require action by governments.'[23] The kind of government action required includes: shifts in how and how long we work (taking into account both paid and unpaid labour in the home); changes to how we plan our cities and towns; the creation of more safe public spaces and more reliable and affordable public transport; improvements to the way our public health system identifies and supports those at greatest risk of diet-related diseases; ensuring greater access to affordable fresh foods for those living in remote corners of Australia; and, most importantly, recommitting ourselves as a nation to eradicating economic and social disadvantage. Only when these projects are attempted can we address the issues of personal choice and willpower that so many diet gurus, gourmands and politicians blame for our poor eating habits and expanding waistlines. As food historian Michael Symons observes, 'Australians now eat both much better and much worse' than we did twenty years ago. 'With so much good food around and with even more bad,' Australian food culture has become increasingly polarised.[24] We need to work towards creating a republic of food in which everyone, regardless of social class, race or sex, is nourished and sustained by what Australia has to offer.

Acknowledgements

Thanks to Louise Wagner, Emily Lee-Ack, Libby Turnock, Ben Dalton and all the guys at He Cooks, Rosanna Scutella, Meredith Curnow, Ken Wyatt, Clare Drysdale, Jennice Kersh, Adam Badenoch, Alex Nahlous, Iain Giblin, Michael Butterworth, Janet Caincross, Norma Ingram, Rebecca Kaiser, Penny Lawrence, Andrew Connolly, Mark Hebblewhite, Cisca Pena, Peter Sheahan, Jane Cleary, Marijana Milosavljevic, Helen Truby, Ruth Hardie, Luke Harris, Frances Parker, Hans van Leeuwen, Dylan Moran (for the chapter title), Cate Thill (for research support), Rae Cooper (for giving me Felipe Fernández-Armesto's book *Food: A History*, which started me thinking), Maggie Hamilton, Jo Paul, Natasha Cica, David Dale, Hugh Mackay, Varuna, The Writers' House (its staff and my fellow housemates Kate, Anne, Felicity and John).

Special thanks to Jean Duruz and Carol Johnson, and to Ipsos Australia for their support, particularly Nicole Torkar, Bill Nicolovski, Dorothy Dudley and Samantha Headland.

I am particularly grateful to Black Inc., Chris Feik and Denise O'Dea.

Thanks, as always, to my sous-chef, Daniel.

ENDNOTES

Introduction: 'Welcome to Australia!'

1   Ian Britain, 'Food for Thought,' *Meanjin: On Food & Drink* 61:4 (2002), 3.

2   For example, the Roy Morgan Readership Survey for October 2005 to September 2006 showed magazines such as *Good Taste* and *Delicious* enjoyed readership numbers of 653,000 and 425,000 respectively, sometimes double the readership numbers of popular women's magazines such as *Vogue* and *Madison*. In addition, there are currently nine titles in the 'entertaining' category for non-weeklies, more than the number of titles in the women's lifestyle, sport, kids and business and financial categories. Consider also that other titles outside the entertainment category, such as those in the homemaker, health, fashion and women's lifestyle categories, include food or cooking sections. Even *Australian Vogue* and *InStyle* slip the occasional recipe into their fashion spreads.

3   Booksellers tell me the interest in cookbooks is on the wane. This might be the case, but looking back at the top selling cookbook each year, the numbers remain high. In 2003, *Jamie's Kitchen* was the top selling cookbook at 47,719. The following year it was Donna Hay's *The Instant Cook* at 55,650. *Jamie's Italy* sold 45,615 in 2005 and Oliver outdid himself in 2006, with *Cook with Jamie* selling nearly 80,000 copies.

4   Isabelle de Solier, 'TV dinners: culinary television, education and distinction,' *Continuum: Journal of Media and Cultural Studies* 19:4 (December 2005), 465.

5   Michael Symons, *One Continuous Picnic: A History of Eating in Australia* (Adelaide, Duck Press, 1982), 254.

6   Don Dunstan, *Don Dunstan's Cookbook* (Adelaide, Rigby, 1976), 28.

7   Cherry Ripe, *Goodbye Culinary Cringe* (Sydney, Allen and Unwin, 1993), 202.

8   Barbara Santich, *Looking for Flavour* (Adelaide, Wakefield Press, 1996), 92.

9   'Tetsuya's fifth in world,' *Sydney Morning Herald*, 24 April 2007. Tetsuya's was ranked fifth, Rockpool, thirty-third. See www.theworlds50best.com/2007_list.html.

10 Frances Short, 'Domestic cooking skills: what are they?' *Journal of the HEIA* 10:3 (2003), 13–22. The notion that cooking skills are in decline is not one advocated by Short, who argues instead that they are in transition. For more about this debate, see chapter six, 'Table for One.'

11 Australia pips US as world's fattest nation,' *Sydney Morning Herald*, 20 June 2008. The report, *Australia's Future Fat Bomb*, was published by the Baker Heart Research Institute and is available online at <baker.edu.au>.

12 See Access Economics, *The Economic Costs of Obesity* (Canberra, October 2006). This report was prepared for Diabetes Australia.

13 www.who.org

14 According to the WHO's figures, in 1995, there were an estimated 200 million obese adults worldwide and another 18 million under-five children classified as overweight. As of 2000, the number of obese adults had increased to over 300 million.

15 Joanna Blythman, *Bad Food Britain: How a Nation Ruined its Appetite* (London, Fourth Estate, 2006), xiii.

16 Blythman, xiii.

17 Blythman, 3–4.

18 Blythman, 9. According to Blythman, research has found that only 20 per cent of British viewers believe TV food programs encourage them to cook. See also Blythman, xvi.

19 No Australian work to date has been done on whether TV cooking shows actually teach people to cook. However, British research

has shown that while viewers saw cooking shows as primarily entertainment, 19 per cent found these shows useful to learn about cooking in later life. See de Solier, 'TV Dinners,' 468.

20 Marian Halligan, 'A cook's life,' *Griffith Review 5: Addicted to Celebrity*, Spring 2004, 256. Fundamentally Halligan takes a jaundiced view of the celebrity chef phenomenon, arguing that these cooking shows are mostly about "some famous person telling people eating rubbish how to cook amazing food". See also Marion Halligan, 'Watched Pots' in *Meanjin* 61:4, 143–151.

21 Blythman, 19.

22 Blythman, 27.

23 www.acnielsen.com.au. See also David Dale, *Who We Are: A Snapshot of Australia Today* (Sydney, Allen and Unwin, 2006), 122.

Cheap as Chips

1 See the Australian Bureau of Statistics' census data at www.censusdata.abs.gov.au. This site allows you to search QuickStats according to postcode.

2 Furthermore, the median weekly household income in 2006 was $616, compared with $1,027 in Australia. The median weekly family income was $806, compared with $1,171 nationally. A household is defined as one or more person living in a residence. A family is more than one person living together and related (by birth or by law).

3 In 2006, 26.7 per cent of families in Elizabeth were one-parent families compared to 15.8 per cent in Australia generally.

4 In Elizabeth in 2006, of the occupied private dwellings being rented, 19.9 per cent were rented from a real estate agent and 53.6 per cent were rented from the state housing authority. In comparison, in Australia 50.5 per cent were rented from a real estate agent and 14.9 per cent from a state or territory housing authority.

5 In 2001, 21.2 per cent of the population of Elizabeth was unemployed. There was a youth unemployment rate of 34.4 per cent. See 'Census of Population and Housing: Selected Education and

Labour Force Characteristics for Statistical Local Areas, South Australia, 2001.' www.abs.gov.au.

6   See David Fawcett's first speech (delivered 18 November 2004) on his home page, www.davidfawcett.net.

7   This is Jackman's description of a south-western Sydney caravan park where a young girl, Chloe Hosum, was molested and killed in 2003. See Christine Jackman, 'Chloe, a victim of life on the fringe,' the *Australian*, 15 November 2003.

8   This is also the case internationally, with overweight and obesity now on the rise in low and middle-income countries, particularly in urban areas. The WHO estimates over 115 million in develop-ing countries suffer from obesity-related problems. See www.who. org. See also Raj Patel, *Stuffed and Starved: Markets, Power and the Hidden Battle for the World Food System* (Melbourne, Black Inc Books, 2007) and Ellen Ruppel Shell, *Fat Wars: The Inside Story of the Obesity Industry* (London, Atlantic Books, 2003).

9   See AIHW Bulletin no. 11, December 2003, www.aihw.gov.au/ publications/index.cfm/title/9652.
    There is an increasing amount of research available on the social gradient to obesity in Australia. See, for example, Sharon Friel and Dorothy Broom, 'Unequal society, unhealthy weight,' in Dorothy Broom and Jane Dixon (eds), *The Seven Deadly Sins of Obesity* (Sydney, UNSW Press, 2007). See also Cate Burns, 'A review of the literature describing the link between poverty, food insecurity and obesity with specific reference to Australia,' April 2004, Victor-ian Health Food Insecurity Program, www.vichealth.vic.gov.au.

10 Men in the most advantaged group had significantly lower rates of obesity (12.7 per cent in 2001) than their counterparts in the most disadvantaged group (19.5 per cent in 2001). Interestingly, there was little difference in the rates of overweight for men in the five socio-economic groups.

11 Cate Burns, 'A review of the literature describing the link between poverty, food insecurity and obesity with specific reference to Australia,' VicHealth, April 2004, www.vichealth.vic.gov.au, pp. 16–17.

12 Burns, 16–17.

Endnotes

13 Jonathan Franzen, *The Corrections* (London, Fourth Estate, 2002), 557.

14 See Michael Gard and Jan Wright, *The Obesity Epidemic* (London: Routledge, 2005), from page 67 onwards. Gard and Wright also make the important point that it is simplistic to argue that anti-fat sentiment is a new phenomenon, and that in the past 'fatness' was celebrated as a marker of high status. Rather, "attitudes of different cultures towards fatness during different periods of history have varied widely". Gard, 69.

15 Patel, 3.

16 See, for example, Katrine Baghurst, 'Social status, nutrition and the cost of healthy eating,' *Journal of the HEIA* 10:3 (2003), 39–42.

17 Burns, 15.

18 Burns, 15.

19 Kerry Coleman and Julie Robotham, 'Healthy food too expensive for many,' *Sydney Morning Herald*, 14 December 2006.

20 Note there is conflicting research about whether those living in low income or socially disadvantaged areas face higher food prices. See Burns.

21 See also P. Allotey, R.A. Cummins, A. Kouamé and D. Reidpath, *Social, Environmental and Cultural Contexts and the Measurement of the Burden of Disease: An Exploratory Comparison in the Developed and Developing World.* (Melbourne, Key Centre for Women's Health in Society, University of Melbourne, 2001). These researchers found that low-income areas have three times the density of fast-food outlets per person.

22 Gard, 128.

23 The Nutrition Obesity Lifestyle and Environment (NOBLE) Study is an ongoing, multidisciplinary project being conducted in South Australia, looking at these very questions. They are due to release their findings in 2008. See for example D. Crawford, D. Jolley, A.M. Kavanagh, T. King and G. Turrell, 'Weight and place: a multilevel cross-sectional survey of area-level social disadvantage and overweight obesity in Australia,' *International Journal of Obesity* 30:2 (2006), 1–7.

EATING BETWEEN THE LINES

24 On ways in which the increasing number of homeless youth obtain food, see Sue Booth, 'Eating rough: food sources and acquisition practices of homeless young people in Adelaide, South Australia,' *Public Health Nutrition* 9:20 (2006), 212–218.

25 Booth, 212. The 1995 Australian National Nutrition Survey found 5.2 per cent of adults had run out of or couldn't afford food in the year previous to the survey, with those unemployed (11.3 per cent) and those paying rent or board (15.8 per cent) particularly deprived. For a report on food insecurity of this type in the Wollongong region, see Sally Babbington, 'When there isn't enough to eat: study of clients at AngiCare's emergency relief service in Wollongong' (Sydney: AngliCare Policy Unit, October 2006).

26 See Adele Horin and Matt Wade, 'One million families on the poverty line,' *Sydney Morning Herald*, 8 August 2007. Wade and Horin quote ABS statistics that more than 820,000 children aged under fourteen live in the 1.05 million households that have been classified as having 'low economic resources.' There were signs of severe financial stress among households in the low economic resources category, with one in every eight saying they had gone without meals in the previous twelve months because of a shortage of money.'

Fat Kids

1 Gard and Wright, 17.

2 Julie Robotham, 'Exercise ruled out for overweight children who can barely move,' *Sydney Morning Herald*, 10 March 2006.

3 Mark Metherell, 'Five years to rein in child obesity,' *Sydney Morning Herald*, 28 November 2005.

4 Australian Institute of Health and Welfare (AIHW), 'A rising epidemic: obesity in Australian children and adults,' *Risk Factor Monitoring* (Risk Factors Data Briefing no. 2), October 2004.

5 Catharine Lumby and Duncan Fine, *Why TV is Good for Kids: Raising 21st-Century Children* (Sydney, Pan Macmillan, 2006), 75–79.

6 Gard and Wright, 136.

7   AIHW, 'A rising epidemic.' This is also reported in Broom et al, *The Seven Deadly Sins of Obesity*, 7.

8   Mandy Biggs, 'Overweight and obesity in Australia,' Parliamentary Library E-brief, 3 October 2006. Published online at <www.aph.gov.au>.

9   Jennifer O'Dea, 'Differences in overweight and obesity amongst Australian school children of low and middle/high socio-economic status,' *Medical Journal of Australia* 179 (July 2003), 63. See O'Dea's website for other articles on the connection between socio-economic status and weight in children: <apcen.edfac.usyd.edu.au/staff/odeaj/index.html>. See also Adele Horin, 'Pattern in "overstated" child obesity,' *Sydney Morning Herald*, 22 October 2007.

10 NSW Centre for Overweight and Obesity (2006). *NSW Schools Physical Activity and Nutrition Survey (SPANS) 2004: Short Report* (Sydney, NSW Department of Health, 2006). The SPANS report stated that "children from lower socio-economic areas and those from Middle Eastern backgrounds were more likely to be in an unhealthy weight range". See also chapter 3, for more on the impact of the pressured parenting environment on children's weight, and chapter 4, pp. 76–78, on the impact of place and socio-economic status of children's weight. See also Broom et al, *The Seven Deadly Sins of Obesity*.

11 Martina Boese and Rosanna Scutella, 'The Brotherhood of St Laurence's social barometer: challenges facing Australian youth,' (Melbourne, Brotherhood of St Laurence, August 2006), 6.

12 Gard and Wright, 130.

13 Gard and Wright, 6.

14 Gard and Wright, 19.

15 Margaret Visser, *The Rituals of Dinner: The Origins, Evolution, Eccentricities and Meaning of Table Manners* (New York, Penguin, 1991), 3.

16 See '"Fat camps" not fit for kids,' *Sydney Morning Herald*, 13 January 2004.

17 Mark Metherell, 'ALP plans childhood obesity checkups', *Sydney Morning Herald*, 11 April 2007.

18 Australian Medical Association, 'ACMA review should lead to ban on junk-food advertising to kids,' media release, 27 June 2007. Available online at <www.ama.com.au>.

19 Jennifer O'Dea and Rachel Wilson, 'Socio-cognitive nutrition factors associated with body mass index in children and adolescents,' *Health Education Research* 26:1 (2006), 10.

20 Gard and Wright, 66.

21 'Hi-5 shocked by childhood obesity rates,' *National Nine News*, 31 August 2006 <http://news.ninemsn.com.au/article.aspx?id=126525>. The article was subsequently posted in a Hi-5 Fanclub online forum, prompting some debate: <www.hi5.com.au>, 31 August 2006.

22 For example, see http://www.health.nsw.gov.au/obesity/adult/canteens/faqs.html and http://www.ncahs.health.nsw.gov.au/docs/tooty_fruity/classroom/fruitbreaks.pdf.

23 See http://education.qld.gov.au/schools/healthy/food-drink-strategy.html.

24 Nicola Humble, *Culinary Pleasures: Cookbooks and the Transformation of British Food* (London, Faber, 2005), 230.

Family Dinners

1 For further insights into the impact of divorce on family eating, see Bruce Smyth and Ilene Wolcott, 'Food and family transitions: cooking in the aftermath of divorce,' *Journal of the HEIA* 11:3 (2004).

2 Visser, 22.

3 Visser, 54, 49.

4 Visser, 55.

5 Visser, 149. Visser makes the point that in other cultures, men, women and children often eat separately, on the floor or from trays, at different times and so forth.

6 Hugh Mackay, *The Wrap: A Distillation of the Key Themes from Twenty-Five Years of the Mackay Report* (Sydney, Mackay Research, 2003), 15.

7 Bob Ashley, Joanne Hollows, Steve Jones and Ben Taylor, *Food and Cultural Studies* (London, Routledge, 2004), 127.

8   Elspeth Probyn, *Carnal Appetites; SexFoodIdentities* (London, Routledge, 2000), 37.

9   Ashley, 124. Consider, too, the following comment from the *Mackay Report* on food, published in 1989: 'In spite of our great propensity for take-away food, and for eating out, "home" is still the ultimate focal point for our preferred eating occasions. We need to remember that, in a society characterised by unstable family life, the ideals of home and family are still fundamentally appealing.'

10 Blythman, 88.

11 Mamun et al, "Positive maternal attitude to the family eating together decreases the risk of adolescent overweight", *Obesity Research* 13:8 (2005), 1422–1430. The authors of the study refer to a number of overseas studies making the link between family meals, maternal presence and children's health and weight.

12 Shari L. Gallup, Cheryl Jones Syracuse and Cindy Oliveri, 'What research tells us about family meals,' *Family Tapestries Fact Sheet* (FS 4-03), Ohio State University, 2003.

13 'Jamie Oliver: from jack-the-lad to food campaigner,' *Good Housekeeping*, November 2006, 29–32.

14 Probyn, 36.

15 The Australian Bureau of Statistics' 2006 'Time Use' survey found that 64 per cent of households had purchased at least one meal from a restaurant in the fortnight prior to being surveyed, while 67 per cent had purchased at least one take-away meal.

16 The complete research findings are available at: www.continental.com.au/mealtimesmatter/research.html.

17 In 72 per cent of the households surveyed, the mother was the main meal provider. The mother was more likely to be the main meal provider even when both mother and father worked full-time.

18 Duruz, 'Home cooking, nostalgia and the purchase of tradition,' *Traditional Dwellings and Settlements Review* 12:2 (2001), 26.

19 Duruz, 'Home Cooking,' 29.

20 See Matt Wade, 'Market does the work men won't,' *Sydney Morning Herald*, 1 November 2006. Wade is reporting on a study by

Barbara Pocock, whose ongoing work on the distribution of unpaid work in the home has shown that because men are slow to take on more domestic responsibilities, the market has taken up the slack. Michael Bittman and Jocelyn Pixley came to similar conclusions in *The Double Life of the Family: Myth, Hope and Experience* (Sydney, Allen and Unwin, 1997). See also Janeen Baxter, 'Patterns of change and stability in the gender division of household labour in Australia, 1986–1997,' *Journal of Sociology* 38:4 (2002).

21 Visser, 49.

22 The authors were quoting an expert on this point. Broom et al, *The Seven Deadly Sins of Obesity*, 37. See generally this chapter for the possible effects of time pressures on people's weight.

23 "Chef to Danish Royals quits in disgust,' *Sydney Morning Herald*, 26 May 2006.

24 Symons, *One Continuous Picnic: A History of Eating in Australia*, 2nd edition (Melbourne University Press, 2007), 326.

25 Gallup et al.

Sex in the Kitchen

1 A newspaper article on He Cooks, covering one of its Melbourne classes, also reported that the students were men who had been 'coddled' by women in the kitchen and were thus bereft of cooking skills. The article's author shared their ineptitude. He writes: 'Mum was the first honorary caterer in my life … Jumping the nest, I filled the belly at noodle shops, twenty-first buffets and the pub. Later, like a Red Cross package … my first real girlfriend landed in my lap. She could cook like a sorceress and my bacon was saved.' The writer's father only 'came off the bench on Sundays for bubble-and-squeak.' David Astle, 'Kitchen Confidence,' *Sunday Life*, 24 September 2006, 19–20.

2 Margaret Visser argues that 'in the modern ceremony of the barbecue, there remains an echo of the ancient ritual of the impromptu meal at the scene of the hunt'. Visser, 229. Barbecuing may be cooking, but it is resolutely macho cooking involving the use of

fire and metal, performed outside, the site of the majority of men's unpaid work.

3   Chelminski also notes, in a mere footnote, that to date only four women have ever won three Michelin stars, the top honour. Rudolph Chelminski, *The Perfectionist: Did France's Obsession with Food Kill Its Most Famous Chef?* (London, Penguin, 2005), 107, 116, 195.

4   Anthony Bourdain, *The Nasty Bits* (London, Bloomsbury, 2006), ix.

5   Bourdain, 7.

6   Andrew Clark, 'Chef turns up the heat on women in the kitchen,' *Sydney Morning Herald*, 25 October 2005.

7   Even the usually snaggy Jamie makes the odd sexist comment along these lines. In the final episode of *Jamie's Kitchen* in Melbourne, he addresses his students via video conference and tells one of the hopefuls that while she might not make the grade at *fifteen*, she could have a great future as a 'female cook.'

8   See Clark. This is also the case with apprenticeships and traineeships in the food and hospitality industry, which interestingly have the highest rates of non-completion across all industries.

9   Barbara Santich, 'It's a chore: women's attitudes towards cooking,' *Australian Journal of Nutrition and Dietetics* 52:1 (1995), 11–13.

10 There were popular and important Australian male celebrity chefs like Bernard King and Ian Parmenter. However, there was always something a bit flamboyant about them that ensured they were far beyond the typical Australian male ideal. Even Peter Russell Clark with his ockerism remained a bit suspect.

11 Bellman, quoted in de Soliers, 472. Note the Lifestyle Channel is now Lifestyle Food, totally devoted to food and cooking programs.

12 de Soliers, 477.

13 Keith Floyd was one of the original bachelor chefs, "an ageing, rakish bon viveur," "the kind of man who likes to show off his cooking skills at high profile events but doesn't like to muck in with everyday domestic cooking." Blythman, 8.

14 See www.abc.net.au/surfingmenu, downloaded 27 October 2006.

15 Joanne Hollows, 'The bachelor dinner: masculinity, class and cooking in *Playboy*, 1953–1961,' *Continuum: Journal of Media and Cultural Studies* 16:2 (2002), 143, 146, 151–152, 146. See also Joanne Hollows, 'Oliver's twist: leisure, labour and domestic masculinity in *The Naked Chef*,' *International Journal of Cultural Studies* 6:2 (2003), 229–248.

16 It should also be noted that while there are few alternative male role models in the celebrity chef world, there is also a dearth of alternative female ones. Most female celebrity chefs fit the comforting or sexy mum role. Gay Bilson and Kylie Kwong are the notable exceptions here.

17 Hollows, 'The bachelor dinner,' 146.

18 'Homecook Hero,' Good Living, *Sydney Morning Herald*, 12 September 2006.

19 See ABS, Australian Social Trends 2001 4102.0, 'Unpaid Work: Time spent on unpaid household work,' www.abs.gov.au. Overall Australians of both sexes are spending less time on housework. Since 1986, women's time spent on housework has declined by six hours per week. However, as Baxter argues, "while the gender gap between men's and women's involvement in the home is getting smaller, it is not the result of men increasing their share of the load, but is due to the large decline in women's time spent on domestic labour." See Baxter, 'Patterns of change and stability in the gender division of household labour in Australia, 1986–1997,' *Journal of Sociology* 38:4 (2002), 399–424.

20 Time spent on food-related chores is down for both men and women since 1997, when 93 per cent of women and nearly 61.7 per cent of men reported participating in food preparation or clean-up. See ABS, Australian Social Trends 2001 4102.0, 'Unpaid Work.' See also HREOC, 'It's About Time: women, men, work and family,' Final Paper, 2007, www.humanrights.gov.au/sex_discrimination/its_about_time/. Men spent an average of thirty-eight minutes per day on housework; women, an average of one hour and thirty-seven minutes. The ABS's 2006 Time Use survey

also found that in general, women employed full-time did more housework than men employed full-time. Interestingly, these surveys have shown that since 1992 men's involvement in food preparation has increased by four minutes per day, while women's involvement has decreased by three minutes.

21 Susan Sheridan, 'Eating the other: food and cultural difference in the *Australian Women's Weekly* in the 1960s,' *Journal of Intercultural Studies* 21:3 (2000), 327.

22 See de Soliers, 469. Nigella has been described as a post-feminist icon. See Joanne Hollows, 'Feeling like a domestic goddess: post-feminism and cooking,' *Cultural Studies* 6:2 (2003), 179–202.

23 See Hollows, 'The bachelor dinner,' 151.

24 See Santich, 'It's a chore.' Interestingly, Santich discovered an age-distinction in attitudes to cooking; women aged fifty and over tended to enjoy cooking, but only half of the younger women surveyed said they enjoyed the task.

25 Ian Matthews, 'Cooking up a storm,' *Sydney Morning Herald*, 30 July 2004.

26 See Barbara Pocock, 'Work and family futures: how young Australians plan to work and care,' The Australia Institute, Discussion Paper No. 69, August 2004. See also Chilla Bulbeck's work on gender issues and the women's movement at her university website, www.adelaide.edu.au. See also Wade, 'Market does the work men won't.'

27 Probyn, 4.

28 Richard Books, 'Jamie Oliver calls for sex ban to get men cooking,' *Sunday Times*, 25 May 2008.

Table for One

1 See ABS, *Australian Social Trends 2005* and *Home Alone*, the Ipsos Mackay Report no. 118, December 2005, 7–8.

2 Symons, *One Continuous Picnic*, 333.

3 ABS, *National Health Survey: Summary of Results* 2004–05, 42.

4 *Home Alone*, 4.

5 *Home Alone*, 23.

6 *Home Alone*, 24.
7 Visser, 4.
8 *Home Alone*, 26.
9 Visser, ix.
10 Visser, 3.
11 Ashley, 125.

Bush Tucker No More

1 The Redfern-Waterloo Authority was established by an act of NSW parliament in 2004 and is responsible for developing the suburbs of Redfern, Waterloo, Eveleigh and Darlington. See <www.redfernwaterloo.com.au>. While the authority proclaims that it will take into consideration 'Aboriginal community needs,' the authority and the minister responsible, Frank Sartor, have been subject to much criticism from locals and the media as well as accusations that it will allow probate development to push out public housing residents, including indigenous ones. See Debra Jopson, Gerard Ryle and Darren Goodsir, 'Revealed: how Redfern will be reborn,' *Sydney Morning Herald*, 29 November 2004.
2 For the history of kangaroos harvesting, management and use see <www.environment.gov.au/biodiversity/trade-use/wild-harvest/kangaroo>.
3 Symons, *One Continuous Picnic*, 49–50.
4 See James Boyce, *Van Diemen's Land* (Melbourne, Black Inc. Books, 2008), 112–113.
5 Beckett, *Convicted Tastes: Food in Australia* (Sydney, Allen and Unwin, 1984), 8.
6 Barbara Santich, 'Eating in Australia: from rations to ravioli,' *Echo*, 14:1 (2002), 24.
7 See Jane Robbins and John Summers, 'Aboriginal affairs policy' in Summers, Woodward and Parkin (eds), *Government, Politics, Power and Policy in Australia*, 7th edition (Sydney, Longman, 2002), 501–526.
8 Keating's Redfern Park speech was delivered on 10 December 1992 and is reproduced in Michael Fullilove (ed), *'Men and Women*

of Australia!: Our Greatest Modern Speeches (Sydney: Vintage, 2005), 157–160.

9 Jennice Kersh and Raymond Kersh, *Edna's Table* (Sydney: Hodder and Stoughton, 1998), 36.

10 Ripe, 198.

11 Kersh and Kersh, 43.

12 Ripe, 197.

13 All this aside, there are still signs of life in the bush food industry. Indigenous food remains interesting to international visitors and overseas markets. For example, Ward McKenzie and Robins Foods, the makers of Australia's leading indigenous goods range, Outback Spirit, formed a partnership in 2006 to take bush foods like wattle seeds, Kakadu plums, lemon myrtle and wild lime to an international market (see 'Bush tucker goes global,' *Koori Mail*, 15 March 2006). On the Australian restaurant scene, Vic Cherikoff is still marketing native food and his bush food restaurant Lillipilli on King is still operating in Sydney. TV chef Mark Olive, aka 'The Black Olive,' appears on ABC-TV's *Message Stick* and the Lifestyle Channel's *Outback Café*; on both programs, he works with bush ingredients. There have seen some examples of Australian food manufacturers using bush foods. Dick Smith uses rosella flower, wattle seed and lemon myrtle in his 'Bush Foods' breakfast cereal. Bush herbs are available at some up-market Coles supermarkets. And in an interesting fusion of science and social work, the CSIRO runs a project at Junee jail where indigenous prisoners help manage a bush food crop that includes bush tomatoes, wattle seed and desert limes. See www.cse.csiro.au/research/nativefoods /crops/bushtomatoes and 'A new sentence for growing in the wild', *Sydney Morning Herald*, 16 May 2003.

14 See the *Australian Institute of Health and Welfare Bulletin* 11 (December 2003).

15 ABS, National Aboriginal and Torres Strait Islanders Social Survey (NATSISS), 2002.

16 See NATSISS 2002.

17 ABS, National Aboriginal and Torres Strait Islanders Health Survey (NATSIHS), 2004–05.

18 Eirick Saethre, 'Nutrition, economics and food distribution in an Australian Aboriginal community,' *Anthropological Forum* 15:2 (2005), 153.

19 Nicolas Rothwell, *Another Country* (Melbourne, Black Inc. Books, 2007), 125.

20 Rothwell, p. 127.

21 Ruppel Shell, 160.

22 Ruppel Shell, 152.

23 On health benefits of the hunter-gatherer diet see Richard M. Smith and Pamela A. Smith, 'An assessment of the composition and nutritional content of an Australian Aboriginal hunter-gatherer diet,' *Australian Aboriginal Studies* 2 (2003), 39–51.

24 Symons, *One Continuous Picnic*, 5–7.

25 Elsie Heiss, diabetes educator, quoted in 'La Perouse yarns up,' *Koori Mail*, 7 April 2004.

26 Symons, *One Continuous Picnic*, 5.

27 Wendy Foley, 'Tradition and change in urban indigenous food practices,' *Postcolonial Studies* 8:1 (2005), 25. On the effect of colonisation on indigenous food practices see pp. 25–26 of this article.

28 Rothwell, 131.

29 Beckett, 8–9.

30 Symons, *One Continuous Picnic*, 5.

31 Beckett, 9.

32 See ABS, NATSIHS 2001.

33 Foley, 25–44.

34 There is some research that suggests indigenous people, both in urban and remote areas, are more reliant on take-away than non-indigenous people. See Saethre, 156.

35 *Overcoming Indigenous Disadvantage: Key Indicators 2005*, report of the steering committee for the review of government service provision (Canberra: Commonwealth of Australia, 2005), 3.42.

36 'Kowanyama residents angry over food prices,' *Koori Mail*, 21 April 2004.

37 See Stephen Leeder and Karen Webb, 'New Year's resolution: let's get rid of excessive food prices in remote Australia,' *Medical*

Journal of Australia 186:1 (2007), 7–8. A review of the last five years of articles in the *Koori Mail* also shows that food prices in remote communities are an issue across the nation.

38 Saethre quotes 1995 statistics that show that in the Northern Territory between 80 and 95 per cent of all food consumed by indigenous communities is bought at the local store or take-away. Saethre, 156.

39 Saethre, 155–157, 160–161.

40 Alice Walker, *Now Is the Time to Open Your Heart* (New York: Random House, 2004), 169–170.

41 Desiree Bissett, 'Bush tucker is best,' *Koori Mail*, 15 Jan 2003.

42 'Bush tucker in the hospitals,' *Koori Mail*, 15 March 2006, 18.

43 For example, eight community stores joined forces to make up the Mai Wiru stores group in central Australia. See 'Fresh food at last!', *Koori Mail*, 12 April 2006.

44 There is some evidence that mainstream public health messages regarding good nutrition are often culturally inappropriate to indigenous people. Jodi Hoffman, 'Healthy eating makes sense,' *Koori Mail*, 13 November 2002. Norma believes that the preventative health messages are not penetrating remote communities. Ken puts this down to language and education. 'There is an assumption that everyone reads and comprehends standard Australian English. It's wrapped around every food package in the shop. But if you can't read, your education level doesn't go above Year 10, you are not able to make informed decisions. You will be faced with that wall of breakfast cereal and you won't be able to work out why the rolled oats is better than the Coco Pops.'

45 Rothwell, 126.

46 A detailed study of costs and incomes in a remote indigenous community in South Australia found that basic living costs consumed up to 85 per cent of family incomes, with food accounting for 35 per cent of the total. In contrast, Australians in general spend less than 20 per cent of the family income on food. See Leeder and Webb, 7.

47 Probyn, 115 and 101–123.

48 Beckett, 8.

Lebs Make the Best Lamb

1 'Aussie Rules,' *Insight*, SBS Television, 19 September 2006.
2 Patrick White quoted by Alan Frost in 'From the Red Country,' in *The Best Australian Essays 2006*, edited by Drusilla Modjeska (Melbourne, Black Inc. Books, 2006), 6.
3 Dunstan, 28.
4 Ripe, ix, 6 and 7–21 ('The Asianisation of the Australian palate').
5 Letters to the editor, *Delicious*, August 2005.
6 Ben Smithhurst, 'The Mufti,' *FHM*, October 2006. Of course, the drunken Aussie yobbo yearning for a kebab is not unlike the British lager lout who routinely scoffs a vindaloo with his mates at the local Indian after the pub shuts. See Ashley, 83.
7 Note that the most popular take-away food, according to this study, was still the humble sandwich. See 'Chips are down in fast food,' *Sydney Morning Herald*, 14 March 2006.
8 See also Katherine Betts and Bob Birrell, 'Australians' attitudes to migration,' *IPA Review* 53:4 (December 2001), 3–5 and Katherine Betts, 'Migrants' attitudes to immigration in Australia: 1990 to 2004,' *People and Place* 13:3 (2005).
9 Academics Effy Alexakis and Leonard Janiszewski have written about the phenomenon of the country 'Greek café,' which enjoyed a golden age from the mid 1930s to the late 1960s in country New South Wales, Victoria and Queensland. These cafés were owned and staffed by Greek men and woman but served familiar Anglo fare such as steak and eggs, chops and eggs, mixed grills and fish and chips. As Alexakis and Janiszewski comment, these Greek café-owners served Aussie-style food rather than the food of their culture because Greek food was for the family home, not the café table. It wasn't until the late 1970s and early 1980s that 'these foods well and truly emerged from behind closed doors to become an accepted part of the Australian palate.' Effy Alexakis and Leonard Janiszewski, 'California dreaming: the "Greek café" and its role in the Americanisation of Australian eating and social habits,' *Modern Greek Studies, Australia and New Zealand: A Journal for Greek Letters* 11–12 (2003–2004), 194.

10 Dunston, 27. See also Symons, *One Continuous Picnic*, chapter 5, 'The Chinese exception.'

11 Alexakis and Janiszewski, 188, 192.

12 Jean Duruz, 'Eating at the borders: culinary journeys,' *Society and Space* 23 (2005), 51–69.

13 See Ghassan Hage in *home/world: Space, Community and Marginality in Sydney's West* (Sydney: Pluto Press, 1997), 121.

14 Hage, *home/world*, 118. See also Hage's reading of 'Molly O'Drew's Eureka Stew,' a children's story in which a potato-based casserole is enriched when a few exotic ingredients are thrown in by various ethnic characters. While everyone adds ingredients only 'one person is allowed the monopoly over cooking from the beginning of the story until its end: the White Australian.' Who happens to be a woman, mind you! Hage, *White Nation: Fantasies of White Supremacy in a Multicultural Society* (Sydney: Pluto Press, 1998), 119–120.

15 Hage, *home/world*, 119.

16 Hage, *home/world*, 99, 119. Symons acknowledges this point, observing that the rise of ethnic food has as much to do with fashions in travel as with immigration trends. See Michael Symons, *A Shared Table: Ideas for an Australian Cuisine* (Canberra, AGPS, 1993), 52–53. Cherry Ripe similarly argues that Baby Boomers' travel experiences in the 1970s exposed them to ethnic tastes. This was further 'compounded by the fact that cheap restaurants where young people could afford to eat' were often those selling 'ethnic' food. Ripe, 13.

17 Hage, *home/world*, p. 136.

18 Bob Hodge and John O'Carroll, *Borderwork in Multicultural Australia* (Sydney: Allen and Unwin, 2006), 166.

19 Sheridan, 180..

20 Hage, *home/world*, 134.

21 Duruz, 'Eating at the borders,' 66. Duruz argues that the radical potential for ethnic cooking and eating to bring about richer culture understanding lies in a process of exchange and learning, in 'mundane intimate exchanges between women across cuisines and cultures, based on moments of interactivity and reciprocity.' Duruz, 'From Malacca to Adelaide,' conference paper, 9.

22 Farah Farouque, Andrea Petrie and Daniella Miletic, 'Minister cuts African refugee intake,' the *Age*, 2 October 2007.

23 John Dickie, *Delizia! The Epic History of the Italians and their Food* (London: Hooder and Stoughton, 2007), 232.

Where Has All the Lettuce Gone?

1 Laura Barton, 'Any samphire?' the *Guardian*, 12 May 2005.

2 Woolworths recorded price increases of as much as 18 per cent in some regional NSW stores, but credited this regional discrimination to 'freight costs and competition.' See Kelly Burke, 'NSW shoppers paying more at the supermarket,' *Sydney Morning Herald*, 2 July 2007. It should be noted that the CHOICE study also found that a single suburb could host both cheap and expensive food options; the New South Wales suburb of Castle Hill was the home of the second most expensive supermarket in Sydney as well as one of the cheapest.

3 'Local food' refers to products that are locally grown, especially those with regional historic and/or cultural significance. 'Local food networks' include community gardens, food co-ops and farmers' markets. For more information about local foods in Australia, see <www.communityfoods.org.au>.

4 Andrea Gaynor, *Harvest of the Suburbs: An Environmental History of Growing Food in Australian Cities* (Perth, University of Western Australia Press, 2006), 1. Gaynor's interest is in the history of 'backyard farming' rather than peri-urban farming, which is the focus of my interest here.

5 Barry McGowan, 'Chinese market gardens in southern and western New South Wales,' *Australian Humanities Review* 36 (July 2005).

6 Frances Parker and Sheryl Jarecki, 'Transitions at the rural/urban interface: "moving in", "moving out" and "staying put",' paper presented to the State of Australian Cities National Conference, 3–5 December 2003.

7 Frances and her students were convinced that due to these language issues, pesticides were not being used correctly by these

market gardeners. Frances Parker, 'The case of Sydney's tainted food scandal,' *The Drawing Board: An Australian Review of Public Affairs* 2(3), March 2001, 151–165.

8   For more on the impact of development on gardens in the Sydney Basin, see Elizabeth Farrelly, 'How do you cook Kellyville max?' *Sydney Morning Herald*, 15 November 2006 and 'Bye Bye Bok Choy!' *Street Stories*, ABC Radio National, 6 July 2005.

9   See www.metrostrategy.nsw.gov.au. For further information on the South-West Growth Centre see http://www.gcc.nsw.gov.au/the-growth-centres/south-west-growth-centre.aspx. The website says this area has the capacity for 115,000 new homes.

10 Ian Sinclair, 'A view from the edge: issues in rural and metropolitan fringe planning,' *New Planner* 49 (December 2001).

11 See also 'Bye Bye Bok Choy' for further interviews with market gardeners in Christina's area.

12 See Paul Bibby, 'Still farming in the city, after all these years', *Sydney Morning Herald*, 13 October 2007.

13 George Morgan, Cristina Rocha and Scott Poynting, 'Grafting cultures: longing and belonging in immigrants' gardens and backyards in Fairfield,' *Journal of Intercultural Studies* 26:1–2 (February–May 2005), 93–105.

14 'Bye Bye Bok Choy!'.

15 In our February Ipsos Mackay Report on corporate responsibility, we found that consumers appear to be making a greater effort to buy Australian-grown food. This trend is being driven by numerous factors, including concern for the plight of local farmers, concerns about the safety and quality of imported food and, for some, concern about 'food miles' and the environmental impact of transporting food long distances.

Basic Meals for the Ultra Rich

1   The OFA is the industry's peak body and represents those working across the organic supply chain: producers, consumers, certifiers, traders, manufacturers and other stakeholder groups. See <www.ofa.org.au>.

2 Julian Lee, *How Good Are You? Clean Living in a Dirty World* (Sydney, Willian Heinemann), 2008: 47–48.

3 These figures were given to me by the OFA.

4 These food prices were registered on the same day, 26 April 2007, to avoid the problem of seasonal price fluctuations.

5 Michael Harden, 'Hard to swallow,' the *Age*, 22 August 2006. For more on the economic, social and cultural drivers associated with buying (or shunning) organic food, see Peter Singer and James Mason, *The Ethics of What We Eat* (Melbourne, Text, 2006).

6 Andrea Gaynor, *Harvest of the Suburbs: An Environmental History of Growing Food in Australian Cities* (Cambridge, Harvard University Press, 1984).

7 See www.macrowholefoods.com.au.

8 Harden, 'Hard to swallow.'

9 See www.coles.com.au/youlllovecoles/organic-products/.

10 In Eric's view, one of the biggest barriers is integrity in accreditation. Is this can of beans really organic? Or am I paying for the label? Eric confessed: 'I go into an organic store and look at all the products on the shelves and think, "Are they all organic"? I have no idea. I have to trust the retailer.'

11 Hélène Cherrier, 'Becoming sensitive to ethical consumption behavior: narratives of survival in an uncertain and unpredictable world,' *Advances in Consumer Research* 32 (2005), 600–604.

12 'Is this a new-age renaissance in food?' B&T, 8 April 2002.

13 There are a few reports of school canteens making the move to organic, albeit in select schools in inner-city suburbs like Sydney's Newtown and Surry Hills, where parents would already be converts to the cause. See Harriet Alexander, 'Lean and green organic canteen a high-school hit,' *Sydney Morning Herald*, 17 February 2007.

14 Ashley et al, 117.

15 Symons, *One Continuous Picnic*, 319.

16 David Brooks, *Bobos in Paradise: The New Upper Class and How They Got There* (New York, Simon and Schuster, 2000), 10.

17 In some ways, the Bobo is the modern day version of Bourdieu's teacher: bourgeois in his social standing, rich in cultural capital,

someone who goes for both exoticism and populism in his cultural, especially culinary, choices. See Pierre Bourdieu, *Distinction: A Social Critique of the Judgement of Taste* (Cambridge, Harvard University Press, 1984), 185.

18 Brooks, 55–58. For a more scathing description of the Bobo food world in the United Kingdom, see Blythman, 2.

19 As Symons points out, 'Versions of the true Parisian restaurant, which elevated dining to an art, arrived here in the early 1950s'. *One Continuous Picnic*, 131. See also p.258 onwards on the influence of French cooking in Australia in the 1960s and 1970s.

20 See www.elbulli.com.

21 Brooks, 82.

22 Brooks, 82.

23 Jean Duruz, '*Cuisine nostalgie*? Tourism's romance with "the rural",' *Communal/Plural* 7:1 (1999), 97–107. In this way, the desire for the exotic meals of migrants is linked, somewhat ironically, to the nostalgia for country and 'home' cooking. Duruz makes this point in a number of her articles. Both involve a retreat into an imaginary food culture, one cosmopolitan and the other parochial. Both are alluring and romantic, and both are premised on suppressing a range of social inequalities and unpalatable truths.

24 Jean Duruz, 'Rewriting the village: geographies of food and belonging in Clovelly, Australia,' *Cultural Geographies* 9:4 (2002), 377.

25 Symons, *One Continuous Picnic*, 262.

26 The Ipsos Mackay Report, 'Premium brands, luxury products,' Feburary 2006.

27 Brooks, 85.

28 Brooks, 85.

Conclusion: Republic of Food

1 Judith Brett and Anthony Moran, *Ordinary People's Politics: Australians Talk about Life, Politics and the Future of their Country* (Melbourne, Pluto Press, 2006), 109.

2 Patel, 3.

3 See, for example, Catholic Social Services Australia, *Dropping Off The Edge: The Distribution of Disadvantage in Australia*, 26 February 2007, at <www.australiandisadvantage.org.au>. That report found that just 1.7 per cent of postcodes and communities across Australia account for more than seven times their share of the major factors that cause intergenerational poverty. See also Australian Council for Social Services, *Australia Fair Report 2007*, at <www.australiafair.org.au>.

4 See *The Ipsos Mackay Report*'s 'Mind & Mood' studies for both 2006 and 2007.

5 Alison McClelland, *No Child … Child Poverty in Australia* (Melbourne, Brotherhood of St Laurence, 2000) at <www.bsl.org.au>.

6 The difference in figures here depends on which measurement for poverty is used. It is 9.9 per cent if you apply the most austere poverty line widely used in international research, adopted by the OECD, which is set at $249 per week. If you apply the poverty line used to define poverty in Britain, Ireland and the European Union, which amounts to $298 per week, then the 19.8 per cent figure is more accurate. See ACOSS's *Australia Fair 2007* report and Peter Saunders, Trish Hill and Bruce Bradbury, *Poverty in Australia: Sensitivity Analysis and Recent Trends* (Sydney: Social Policy Research Centre, University of New South Wales, 2007).

7 See Senate Community Affairs Reference Committee, *A Hand up Not a Hand out: Renewing the Fight against Poverty* (Canberra, Commonwealth of Australia, 2004).

8 See Australian Bureau of Statistics, 'Paid work: longer working hours,' *Social Trends 2003*, 4102.0, www.abs.gov.au. See also RMIT's Iain Campbell's work on Australians working long hours and performing more unpaid overtime. Iain Campbell, 'Long working hours in Australia: working-time regulation and employer pressures,' *The Economic and Labour Relations Review* 17(2) 2007, 37–68.

9 Dorothy H. Broom, Rennie M. D'Souza, Lyndall Strazdins, Peter Butterworth, Ruth Parslow and Bryan Rodgers, 'The lesser evil: bad jobs or unemployment? A survey of mid-aged Austral-

ians,' *Social Science and Medicine* 63 (2006), 575–586.

10 Australian Institute of Health and Welfare, 'Are all Australians gaining weight?: differentials in overweight and obesity among adults, 1989/90 to 2001,' *Australian Institute of Health and Welfare Bulletin* 11 (December 2003).

11 Visser, 354.

12 This was one of the key findings in the *Ipsos Mackay Report*, 'Premium Brands Luxury Goods', February 2006.

13 Alan Saunders, 'Cooking with love,' the *Monthly*, December 2006, 74–76.

14 Blythman, 7.

15 Anne Manne, 'Love Me Tender?' in *The Best Australian Essays 2007*, edited by Drusilla Modjeska, (Melbourne, Black Inc. Books, 2007), 251.

16 Quoted in New South Wales Centre for Public Health Nutrition, *Food Security Options Paper* (Sydney, NSW Health, June 2003), 1, see www.health.nsw.gov.au. This is one of the best and most comprehensive reports on how best to handle the food security problems of Australia.

17 See, for example, David Braithwaite, 'Drought to push up food prices,' *Sydney Morning Herald*, 12 December 2006.

18 See the *Ipsos Mackay Report*, 'Mind & Mood,' June 2007.

19 See www.australia2020.gov.au for a round-up of these proposals.

20 Julie Ferry, 'Eat your greens,' the *Guardian*, 7 June 2007.

21 See www.slowfood.com.

22 For example, see www.convivialtimes.com.au and www.slowfood.com.

23 See Clive Barnett, Nick Clarke, Paul Cloke and Alice Malpass, 'The political ethics of consumerism,' *Consumer Policy Review* 15:2 (March/April 2005), 45–51.

24 Symons, *One Continuous Picnic*, 329.

SELECT BIBLIOGRAPHY

Access Economics. *The Economic Costs of Obesity*. Canberra: Access Economics, October 2006.

Australian Bureau of Statistics data can be accessed online at www.censusdata.abs.gov.au.

Australian Council of Social Service. *Australia Fair Report 2007*. Sydney: ACSS, 2007.

Australian Institute of Health and Welfare. *A Rising Epidemic: Obesity in Australian Children and Adolescents*. Canberra: AIHW, 2004.

Australian Institute of Health and Welfare. *Are All Australians Gaining Weight?* Canberra: AIHW, 2003.

Beckett, Richard. *Convicted Tastes: Food in Australia*. Sydney: Allen and Unwin, 1984.

Blythman, Joanna. *Bad Food Britain: How a Nation Ruined Its Appetite*. London: Fourth Estate, 2006.

Britain, Ian (ed.). *Meanjin: On Food and Drink* 61:4 (2002).

Brooks, David. *Bobos in Paradise: The New Upper Class and How They Got There*. New York: Simon and Schuster, 2000.

Broom, Dorothy H. and Dixon, Jane (eds). *The Seven Deadly Sins of Obesity*. Sydney: University of New South Wales Press, 2007.

Gard, Michael and Jan Wright. *The Obesity Epidemic*. London: Routledge, 2005.

Gaynor, Andrea. *Harvest of the Suburbs: An Environmental History of Growing Food in Australian Cities*. Perth: University of Western Australia Press, 2006.

Human Rights and Equal Opportunities Commission. *It's About Time: Women, Men, Work and Family*. Sydney: HREOC, 2007.

Ipsos Mackay Reports. *Mind and Mood* (2006, 2007), *Premium Brands, Luxury Products* (2006), *Home Alone* (2005).

Mackay, Hugh. *The Wrap: A Distillation of the Key Themes from Twenty-five Years of the Mackay Report*. Sydney: Mackay Research, 2003.

NSW Centre for Overweight and Obesity. *NSW Schools Physical Activity and Nutrition Survey (SPANS) 2004: Short Report*. Sydney: NSW Department of Health, 2006.

Overcoming Indigenous Disadvantage: Key Indicators 2005. Report of the steering committee for the review of government service provision. Canberra: Commonwealth of Australia, 2005.

Patel, Raj. *Stuffed and Starved: Markets, Power and the Hidden Battle for the World Food System*. Melbourne: Black Inc. Books, 2007.

Probyn, Elspeth. *Carnal Appetites: FoodSexIdentities*. London: Routledge, 2000.

Ripe, Cherry. *Goodbye Culinary Cringe*. Sydney: Allen and Unwin, 1993.

Ruppel Shell, Ellen. *Fat Wars: The Inside Story of the Obesity Industry*. London: Atlantic Books, 2003.

Symons, Michael. *A Shared Table: Ideas for an Australian Cuisine*. Canberra: Australian Government Publishing Service, 1993.

Symons, Michael. *One Continuous Picnic: A History of Eating in Australia*. Adelaide: Duck Press, 1982. Revised edition: Melbourne University Press, 2007.

Vinson, Tony. *Dropping off the Edge: The Distribution of Disadvantage in Australia*, Canberra: Catholic Social Services Australia, 2007.

INDEX

Index